# _The Polygraph Investigators of Luna Pier_

## By Richard Ankony

Dedication:

To my beautiful wife and daughters who are the fulfillment of my life's struggles.

*The Switchman*

*"In these days, I walk the earth with men.  I am the switchman.*

*You don't know me or look at me twice when I walk by you, for I am but a phantom, a ghost and a mere shadow to you.*

*But the day will truly come, when you shall be falsely accused due to circumstances beyond your control.  In that day, you shall be condemned to the dark places and all that you have will be at stake.*

*You will be broken, you shall be shackled, your character will be assassinated and the very essence of your being cast into the pit of hell.*

*You shall be defenseless, helpless, forsaken, crushed and truly lost. Your freedom, your marriage, your family, your work, your money, your health and your life will pass before you like sand blowing in the wind.*

*As you hopelessly sit there, mocked and condemned, you will pray to the heavens for deliverance from your false accusers who have come for your soul.*

*It is in that day that I, the switchman, shall enter into your life and you shall truly see me for what I am.  It is in that day and thereafter, that you will truly know who I am.*

*For you shall put your arms around me and weep on my shoulder and give thanks.*

*For my prime directive is simple, free the souls of the captive innocent, so that they may live and know justice.*

*Indeed, I shall do this, until the end of my days."*

*Richard E. Ankony*
*Polygraph Examiner*

## *Chapter 1 - The Wheel of Fortune*

After a two week vacation, I, Frank Legion, returned for another day in the world of working private investigations and polygraph examinations. Who knows where the thirty years have gone in the polygraph profession with thousands of tests, the fourteen years of private investigations as a private eye or the twenty-five years as a police officer.

Walking down the long hallway towards my office, I wondered if today would be the day that I'd be able to have a cup of coffee, relax in a chair and read the newspaper before getting assigned another examination. I could hear the familiar voice of the office secretary Coco answering calls and stating, "This is Luna Pier Polygraph Services and Private Investigations Inc."

Afterwards a young attractive lady in beachwear came in off the beach and began talking to Coco apparently concerned about her husband's alleged infidelity. The young lady began asking Coco if we handle marital disputes, whereby, Coco replied most definitely. The inquisitive young blonde lady then asked Coco what kind of people would take a polygraph examination?

Coco stated a lot of professional people have taken a polygraph examination for one reason or another. She then stated specifically, "We run examinations on attorneys, prosecuting attorneys, judges, airline pilots, air traffic controllers, mob figures, dope dealers, politicians, Roman Catholic priests, doctors, police officers, politicians and the public at large. We polygraph all criminal, civil, domestic cases and marital cases. We do multi-state travel and we run the examination at your location of preference including your home. All examinations are strictly confidential with attorney client privileges."

The pretty lady looked impressed as she walked out the door stating in passing, she was coming back with her husband.

I started to laugh. "You know Coco, regarding your selling speech, I haven't passed one politician in thirty years of practice, maybe you should warn them."

Coco began laughing, "Who believes a politician anyway, Frank. By the way, you had a call from an Attorney Smith, who wants you to respond to Cain County Jail, Ohio and run a polygraph examination on a client of his who is accused of murder on a drug deal gone bad."

"Drug deal gone bad?" I said, "And now they're asking for justice and mercy Coco. If he did the crime, let him do the time. I mean it was fun until he got caught."

"Well," Coco replied, "apparently his attorney believes he didn't commit a crime but rather thinks it may have been in self-defense."

"Self defense," I laughed, "You know Coco, you got to love these defense attorneys, their clients are always innocent or they acted out of self-defense. Twenty-five years as a street cop taught me something. Bullshit, book'm no bond. Cain County Jail? Damn, I hate going into that lice infested place. You know if you hooked up all those prisoners' heads in series, I don't think they could light up a 40-watt light bulb. I mean some people are made for prison."

While typing an old report of mine Coco stated, "Correct me if I am wrong but aren't polygraph examiners neutral before commencing an assigned polygraph examination, Frank?"

"Coco, your right, but I'm human, okay. I'm always neutral and I've never taken a bribe, even when offered as high as $10,000 to throw a test. Neither do I genuflect in the presence of the powers that be. Yet, I cannot close my mind off from reality. These drug dealers like their way of life, the fast lane, the easy cash and the dolls. As always, its fun until their caught, then they scream for justice and find Jesus.

You know Coco; I may have been born during the day but not yesterday, okay. The common man works his whole life and gets little to nowhere while these bastards drive the big cars corrupt our politicians, destroy society and live the easy life.

Yes, I'll run the test and talk with the attorney, but his client better be given a heads up that he will have to pass his examination on his own volition. I'm not cutting him any slack. By the way are there any more details to this crime?"

Coco checked her note file then stated, "Well, Frank, the attorney was hesitant on giving specific details over the phone but did mention the drug deal went bad under a bridge overpass in Ohio. Apparently guns were pulled and shots were fired at point-blank range within the car, and initially they missed each other. Which is hard to believe, but they did. Yet, they continued firing until the other party who was behind the driver's seat got hit and fell out of the car. I don't know more then that."

"Okay." I responded, "So that's it?"

Coco looking at her notes, "Yes, that's all I got, the attorney didn't want to go into further details because it gets gruesome after that."

"Oh, how's that, Coco?"

"He wouldn't say, Frank."

"You know Coco, I'm going to need the attorney to get clearance for me from the jail administrator in order to run the test. Is he aware of that?"

"He wasn't sure if you did it or he did it, Frank?"

As I lit up my Robusto cigar, "He does it, that's why he gets paid the big bucks, I run polygraph examinations and matters that pertain to the polygraph examination, he does all the legal and paperwork. You know this business is unique; it's the only business that tells attorneys what to do. Anyway, I'll check it out."

Coco responded, "All right, Frank, you got it from here."

Wondering where were all the other examiners, I asked, "Why wasn't Denise or Leila given the assignment? Denise has a police background and good investigative skills while Leila is a digger and keeps pursuing the case until she gets a full confession. It would seem that either one of them would be a perfect fit for this assignment. What's the deal with this? Is this case a man's thing or is it that the ladies don't want to be left alone in a cell with some of those big bucks?"

Coco looked back, "Neither Frank. This came down from the top, the man upstairs wants you to run it."

Smoking my cigar, "Ed?"

"Yes, there's big money in this case Frank." responded Coco; "He wants experience on this one. Besides, Leila is already tied up on an investigation and her cohort in crime Sheila is looking into conducting a polygraph examination in Indiana, for a police department and the attorney general's office.

Furthermore, as I speak, Denise is being dispatched to Toledo, Ohio. She's conducting an investigation at Oregon Federal Prison for Women, regarding a young woman blowing up her husband with a pipe bomb."

"Damn." Shaking my head, "I thought Sheila would rather do investigations and interrogations then polygraph examinations. Indiana? Oh, what's that about?"

"Your going to love this one Frank," Coco laughed, "Sheila, is waiting for the Attorney General to give her the green light for polygraph examinations on a bunch of road police officers, ranking officers, detectives sergeants and union men who claim their superior officer greets them daily by squeezing their penis instead of shaking their hands."

Hearing that, my cigar dropped, "Your shitting me?"

Coco laughing and blushing, "No, the State Attorney General is involved in this case. Apparently, the police supervisor in question refuses to take a polygraph examination regarding this matter. Yet, the plaintiffs are vehemently standing by their story and want to be tested. Matter-of-fact, they are demanding to be tested. They stated they want out of state neutral examiners who are both state licensed and certified. Which is why they chose us instead of Indiana examiners.

Astonishing, as it may seem the police union is allowing the police officers to take the test by waiving all their rights because all of them are willing participants."

Picking my cigar off the floor and laughing, "Damn, that's one hell of a handshake! Like the saying goes, two things raise to the top, the cream of the crop and swamp scum."

"On another note Frank," As Coco was reviewing her notes on her computer screen, "Due to your prior military and civilian explosive bomb training, Denise asked if you could assist her in the bomb case?

Ed and the bomber's attorney agree your assistance would be beneficial."

"Well, Coco, I loved to, but I can't be in two places at once. Tell Denise; I'll do what I can to help her when I break free from my caseload. On another note, Leila called me last night and expressed concern about her case. What's, Leila doing?"

"Apparently since last week," Coco mentioned, "Leila has responded to Indiana and is currently investigating an internal theft case of $250,000 in pennies that a armored car company allegedly claims was stolen from a caged and secure environment in broad daylight."

"That sounds like a zoo to me Coco. What about Doug, Tracy or Kelly and the rest of the gang?"

"All are out on investigations or polygraph examinations. We're so booked, Frank, that we are pulling investigators from Maumee Bay and Bolles Harbor branches. Even our seaway investigator, Darryl, from the Toledo Light House branch has been called in."

"Damn, Coco, it must be a full moon. We're even bringing in Darryl, our best great lake waterway investigator?

Man…business must be picking up; it was dead when I left on vacation two weeks ago.

You got the name and phone number of that attorney that I'm suppose to call?"

Coco shuffling through her papers, "Yes, here it is. Call him today before 5 p.m."

I replied, "Okay, I'm on it Coco."

I couldn't help but think as I responded back to my desk about all the unique cases in the polygraph investigative business with their various degrees of complexity.

It was almost unfathomable how people's destiny hangs on such slender threads.

Life is a mystery; we don't know why we are here, where we are going or where we are from. Yet we are here. It reminds me of my days as a police officer where I like to believe I was amongst the best in arresting mentally disturbed people.

They didn't know where they came from, where they were or where they were going. The only thing that was different between the mentally insane and alleged sane people was that the "mentals" were also a threat to themselves, others and indigent.

While us "proper" people were allegedly not a threat to others or ourselves, on paper. However, with the economy as it is in shambles, it would surely make us indigent. Furthermore, it seems to me the human species is a threat to themselves and others, which would surely qualify us as a mentally deranged species.

For all I know this beautiful orb that floats through void of space known as earth, is really an insane asylum for spiritually deranged spirits. Perhaps that's what happened a long time ago, the universe quarantined us mentally unstable souls by casting us out of heaven and left us to our lonely fate, alone, confused and warlike.

As I snapped out of my dream state and back to business, I made that call to Attorney Smith.

"Yes, hello. I'm, Frank Legion, polygraph examiner, returning a call for Attorney Smith, regarding a murder case. He called Luna Pier Polygraph Services and Private Investigations earlier. Is he in?"

Secretary, "Yes, he is. Please hold."

"Yes, Mr. Legion. This is Attorney Smith, thanks for returning the call so promptly. Mr. Legion, what I have here, according to my client, are two young men who were parked underneath a bridge overpass and were having a few beers while discussing some business. After a short period of time an argument ensued where a fight broke out. Allegedly, at that time they pulled guns on each other and started shooting at point-blank range.

"Counselor, why were they packing guns and what was the argument over?"

"Well, my client Tyrone stated he carried the gun for self-defense purposes and that he was afraid of Reggie, the driver. Tyrone has a murder charge in the first degree pending, yet he maintains that he is innocent because his actions were strictly defensive in nature by trying to protect himself."

"Why would he want to go with Reggie, then? I'm sorry, I was thinking out loud."

"I agree, Mr. Legion. Outside of the fact that my client maintains his innocence any details pertaining to this case are sketchy at best. Tyrone is not telling me much."

"OK, counselor. We'll do our best to get to the truth of the matter as your agent. As always we believe a person is innocent until proven guilty.

When were you looking for the test and where do I send the report?"

"Mr. Legion, I would appreciate it if you ran the test tomorrow at the Cain County Jail, Toledo, Ohio around 1:00 pm, if you could. When the examination is completed please send the report to me A.S.A.P."

"I take it counselor the jail administrator has been notified and advised?"

"Yes, I have advised him and he will be expecting you at that time. I also told the administrator, you're a retired police officer. I'll fax you the clearance if you like."

"Yes, please do counselor. Understand counselor, if your client is troublesome, pugnacious or combative with me, it's an automatic failure. Moreover, if the administrator or your client delays the start of the examination for two hours, I leave and charge full boat."

"Mr. Legion, I understand that time is money. Again, make sure when you generate the report you forward it to me as soon as possible so I can present it to the prosecutor."

"Affirmative counselor, the report will be dispatched the day after the examination. I thank you for the business and I'll be at the jail tomorrow to run the examination."

After working through a bunch of paperwork and relighting my mild smoking cigar. I was starting to feel downright righteous when I decided it was time to meander down Main Street to Dave's Coney Island for grease and chilidogs.

Coco caught me before I could slip out the door, "Frank, before you go for lunch, Ed wants to talk to you upstairs."

Dang, I said to myself, what's this about? "Okay Coco, did you say now or after lunch?"

"He said now, Frank?"

"Okay, I'm on it, Coco."

As I made my way past the front office, down the corridor and up the stairwell, I couldn't help but think how this was going to end someday. I didn't make a killing in this business but it sure was interesting. Every case was unique and intriguing. God I love it, I love it so, more then my life.

*As a cop I learned the heart of America but as a polygraph examiner and private investigator, I learned its soul.*

*No one gets closer but God himself.*

My work crossed the full spectrum of America through interviewing people in their homes who were near billionaires down to people living in the back of a pickup truck whose lives didn't matter since the day they were born.

Polygraph and investigative work with all of its uncertainty had left a deep spiritual scar on my soul. I finished cases troubled after witnessing the deep spiritual emptiness and suffering of people who were very powerful politically and influential down to the "street people." I especially could empathize with the "street people" for they were helpless and nothing more then a voice crying out in the wilderness with no one to help them.

I also knew in my heart that Americans across the board were a just and caring people yet internally they were suffering horribly.

Observing this first hand, I quickly realized that America's fiber, the family structure, was dying before my very eyes. Yes, the family structure was dying without any hope of recovery and it broke my heart to witness this tragic event.

The endless crying I watched, the sorrow, the pain and my helplessness that crushed my soul. The children without fathers, the screaming women whose husbands had given them venereal diseases overwhelmed me at times.

The endless cases I've seen of decent fathers who were going to commit suicide because of the false allegations by their senseless biological daughters who deliberately and falsely accused them of molesting them.

I grieved as I watched the hopelessness and despair of examinees as they explained their suffering and pain who would then walk out into traffic to kill themselves or overdose on drugs when my conclusions weren't favorable.

I've witnessed screaming pregnant women who collapsed on the floor and those who try to stab their fetus because their husbands had confessed to extramarital affairs in front of their father-in-laws.

During confessions I witnessed the hearts of the examinee go into fibrillation or stop "cold."

Then there were those who warned me that they would commit suicide in front of me if their spouse failed their examination.

The captive souls who looked at me with sunken eyes from behind prison bars that pleaded with me saying "Please, don't leave me, don't leave me here to die, save me."

Then the most dreadful scarring of my soul as I gazed upon the haunting eyes of children who looked at me with fear wondering whether they would have a father or mother by the end of the day?

For I have become the "handwriting on the wall," the executioner, for the children's providers have been held in the balance and found wanting.

"Mene.. mene…tekel."

And the guilty soul knew my presence for I could see despair in their eyes for the hour of shadows had come upon them….*for to them, I was death… the destroyer of worlds.*

My soul was crushed and I could find no comfort or refuge, at times. How could I keep this façade of a strong outer character when the very essence of my being was dying and torn asunder from within by watching the endless suffering of so many innocent people?

I ran out of tears long ago as I cried alone in my solitude and emptiness. It was my cross to carry as I stumbled and fell on the road to Calvary…yet I had to get up but where would the strength come from…where?

For on my watch I rectified the lives of the broken and forgotten souls who had no one to turn to and was falsely accused.

Yes I, the *Switchman,* must come…for my soul as if led by an unseen power demanded it.

Throughout my days I would take the time and care to hear the downtroddens testimony. I would sit down with them, comfort them and give them their moment of due.

I would look them in the eyes with compassion and empathize with them in their deep sorrow and helplessness. I tried within every fiber of my alleged harden exterior to make them feel like they were someone and that they were human beings. Even if they were guilty, at the end of the day when the dust settled they would thank me because for the first time in their life someone sat down with them and heard their story.

In their own way, whether guilty or innocent, they tried to tell me again and again, that they were somebody that had a soul and their life did matter.

To my surprise, not even the courts looked at them as a human beings but rather a number, a creature… a thing, which does not deserve to be heard!

To be falsely accused is among the most demoralizing and destructive events cast on humans, for it assassinates one's character and destroys one's soul.

*How well I know the feeling, how well I know the pain.*

It was a damn good feeling to free the captive innocent by breaking their yoke and shackles and prevent them from committing suicide. To send fathers and mothers back to their children and give the hopeless another chance on life…indeed born again….indeed!

Suddenly, I came out of my self-induced hypnotic trance and realized an absolute fact, that I, Frank Legion, made a difference in this world and changed it for the better.

Yes, I, Frank Legion did that, and will do that unto the end of my days.

As I spotted the head man, Ed, in his office with his stack of papers littered over his desk, the smell of cigars filled the air. As I approached him, I could see him looking with his binoculars out across Lake Erie watching the iron ore freighters.

"Ed, Coco, stated you wanted to see me."

"Come on in, Frank. Yes, I'm going to be heading out of town on a business vacation for a couple weeks and I want you to oversee the investigative and polygraph operations that are going on in my absence. You up for that?"

"Sure, Ed, but I have a couple of examinations pending and I was asked to assist Denise with her investigation. Moreover, I have to close up some loose ends and generate a few reports from past cases and investigations."

"No problem, Frank. I need you because of your experience and middle of the road approach. Since you were on vacation we received a hell of a caseload for polygraph examinations and private investigations. Their moneymakers and a lot of these cases are from mid-level to high-level attorneys. All these cases need seasoned investigators and examiners especially on the homicides, as you already know."

"Thank you for the compliment Ed. Yes, I already talked with an Attorney Smith whose client is accused of murder in the first degree. I will be running an exam for Mr. Smith at Cain County Jail tomorrow. When are you leaving and where are you headed?

"Washington D.C. then Florida, Frank. I'll be leaving as soon as I'm finished talking to you. Coco will be informed to forward all information to you and I instructed her to tell the other nine examiners-investigators that you're in charge in my absence."

"Did you say D.C., Ed? Something up?"

"There's something in the wind, Frank."

"Hmm…not at liberty to discuss it, Ed?"

"No, Frank."

"Well, I won't push the issue, Ed, but it sounds international in scope and similar to the last situation we got involved in just after Iraq was invaded.

That *"out of country detail"* conducted near the largest Arab population in North America, was almost disastrous. You know that, the United States Government knows that and so did the White House know that within five minutes of the *uprising*. That domestic detail to obtain the votes and registration for the creation of a new and democratic Iraq was dangerous and volatile. The European Union, the United Nations and our own three letter agencies sent monitors to said location and screened our backgrounds for this detail. In the end, this multinational detail almost cost us our lives. Better stated, it almost cost the lives of about twenty-five seasoned and hardened lawmen along with their multi-degree black belt associates.

It would have been a blood bath if shots were fired, Ed, for hundreds of Iraqi's would have been shot and killed instantly at point-blank range. Our intelligence informed us that some Iraqi's were instigators and some were found with guns on their person within our restricted zone. But despite that, we twenty-five lawmen, all patriots, from different cities, states and federal agencies stood shoulder-to-shoulder with eyes to the front as these three-thousand screaming and violent Iraqi's began chanting in unison with their political black power salute, *"Long Live Saddam Hussein."*

All the while our hands were gradually reaching for our police revolvers and long guns as we locked onto our targets without flinching. I remember how our black belt associates eyes were fixated on their targets, as if jungle cats stalking their prey.

We knew, Ed, that the Iraqi's would have no mercy on us in that moment of time and we also knew that we would have had no mercy on them. Both sides knew that we were in the killing fields and dying time was near.

Imagine that, in our own country, the USA, the Iraqi's were yelling *"Long Live Saddam Hussein,"* Ed, and we were paying, feeding and supporting them. I tell you true Ed, if one of those Iraqi's made one wrong move, just one, there would have been such a massive display of gunfire supported by black ninjas that the country would still be talking about it today.

I can only imagine the volley of fire we would have laid down on them accompanied with flash bangs, CS canisters and gas. Moreover, imagine this hand picked, best of the best ninjas fighting alongside these patriotic lawmen against this Anti-American crowd to the death. God only knows what would have happened, Ed, when the fighting and shooting started.

I can only imagine if the American people heard on television the following day or read in their morning newspaper that fifty or so American patriots, in their country fought to the death defending votes and registration of the birth of the Iraq nation only to be brutally murdered by 3,000 Iraqi's.

I cannot imagine Ed, the terrible anger and the horrible resolve that would have incensed the American people to continue the coalitions destruction of Iraq. For within Americas own border, a battle of the Alamo or *Thermopylae*, if you like, was about to begin and the shedding of blood of their sons was ready to be spilled upon this field of valor.

I remember, Ed, as I stood there targeting six men that I perceived as my last act on earth before I was grabbed from behind. For in the fog of this uprising a three letter agency man came up from behind me, tapped me on my shoulder and with a cold stare stated, "Legion get back upstairs and guard the votes and registrations *at all cost. At all cost, Legion*! No one must tamper with these votes and registration forms, you understand."

I could hear him yell out to the patriots to "Hold the line men and protect the votes." I could hear the radio chatter over the multi-agencies channels calling for all available law enforcement cars to respond to said location for an emergency was in progress.

As I backed my way up the steps with pistol drawn and flash bangs in my hand, I could see national television cameramen who were on the scene being beaten to the ground and their cameras smashed. As I continued to walk backwards down the long dead end corridor, I could hear another three-letter agency man talking on the telephone to White House personnel who already knew that things were going violently wrong.

You know, Ed, it was in that moment of time when I reached the back of that dead-end hall with all my weapons laid out awaiting the final assault that bothered me the most. I realized that if the Iraqi's rushed and overwhelmed these lawmen that most of my brothers would probably be dead and *I would be the last man standing*. I further realized that no one would have ever known what happened to us on that day and they would have wondered how could all these seasoned veterans been cut down, in their own country by an ungrateful people?

In dreadful anticipation I waited for the final assault on my position until finally the Iraqi's blinked. For the Iraqi's had seen death many times in their land and they realized our eyes had scene death and our guns were notched. Though they backed down on that fateful day, the Iraqi's knew we meant business especially when the shotguns were pulled out *along with other weapons*.

You know Ed; in my twenty-five year history as a lawman that *event* was among my finest moments. To stand alongside with those brave men against such overwhelming numbers, is a memory I'll never forget.

In the end two other chosen men and myself where selected from the best of the best to deliver those votes and registrations to Washington D.C., per the White House.

I was there, Ed, at the very conception for the creation of a new and democratic Iraq. You know that entire ride down there Ed, we were armed to the brim, yet we still didn't know if we were going to get hit with a rocket propelled grenade launcher (RPG) or attacked by Saddam`s agents. That extended tractor trailer which carried all the votes and registrations of the free Iraqi people from North America was ground zero for the development of the Iraqi government. I was there, Ed, when we were ordered not to lose site of that tractor-trailer driver at all cost. You know I had to whip out my badge one time to shut down the Washington Gateway expressway because we got separated from the tractor-trailer and we feared Saddam`s agents had come between us. I mean all the vehicles that saw my badge stopped until we caught up to the tractor-trailer. In that moment of time Ed, Washington D.C. and the White House were watching us and I knew that if we called out for help, every single lawman who was available and not on a critical detail would have responded to our location to assist. All in all it was a very moving experience Ed for my associates and myself.

What I'm trying to say Ed in this extended reply is that I don't need another O.K. Corral scenario like this and I don't want another notch on my gun.

So I hope Ed, if your trip in part is about Iran, you'll give me a heads up on it. I would appreciate that very much as a matter-of-fact.

Other then that, I'm ready to take the helm. Enjoy your trip, stay safe and I'll see you on the flip side.

"I apologize what I put you through last time Frank and we appreciate your professional demeanor throughout that Iraq nation building detail. Furthermore, I respect and appreciate what you just told me. It won't happen again and I'll square with you when I return."

"That'll work, Ed."

As I watched Ed leave Luna Pier, I couldn't help but wonder when he would hang it up. Apparently, he was like so many lawmen I knew in police work that died on the throttle, for they felt life is work and without it, life is meaningless.

Ed had worked in Air Force Intelligence just after the Korean War and was a great lover of the polygraph technique as an interrogation tool. It has been an honor to work with him. I consider Ed to be amongst the best of the best in the field of polygraphy. He's been running polygraph examinations from multi-state locations for over fifty years. You would have thought he would have left in his golden years, but no, his life was here.

Many a day Ed and I would walk out on the dock of Luna Pier and talk about white-collar crime and various countermeasures used by criminals to attempt to defeat the polygraph technique. Ed was a believer that the polygraph technique was far more accurate then the 85% to 95% accuracy claimed by the Defense Department and the three-letter agencies. Myself, I would only state what the research claimed though I personally believed theoretically that three-polygraph examiners working on any criminal matter or any civilian case together would be sufficient enough to get to the truth of the matter far quicker and with greater accuracy then any trial by jury or judge.

Matter-of-fact, I was convinced that the polygraph technique was far more efficient in determining truth and deception then the court system. I, like Ed, believed in the polygraph technique coupled with a seasoned investigator as the best interrogation tools on the planet. The polygraph wasn't perfect by any means, but damn it was deadly in the hands of a good examiner. There was many a time that an attorney thought they had all the critical information on their client's case until the polygraph examiner showed up on the scene. After the polygraph examiner briefed them on the newly discovered facts, the attorneys realized that their client gave them nothing but a lie. I couldn't count the times when I would take the attorney's client aside to interrogate his case and within minutes of seeing my polygraph instrument the client would start chattering nonstop like a squirrel on a high wire. There were many times I would walk out of the attorneys office in less then two hours with $1,500 for the company. Funny thing about life, in police work I saw cops practically want to kill you for inadvertently short changing them 5 dollars for their work but these same people would pay $1,500 to the polygraph examiner for less then two hours work…*and thank you.*

The polygraph profession was one of the best little known professions out there, that is, if you could take the heat. The public really didn't know anything about the polygraph technique, let alone understand it. It was surrounded in intrigue and mystery. But it was in that mystery, that we examiners got the admissions, the confessions and the truth of the matter.

Many people were just terrified of the instrument and upon seeing *"the box"*, they would instantaneously start confessing as if they were speaking in tongues or in the final stages of an exorcism.

Though I had double master degrees, men without a college degree in the polygraph profession heydays could make $500,000 a year, unbelievable. All the polygraph examiners I knew were near millionaires to multi-millionaires except for myself because I was tied up in the law enforcement field also.

At the time I got fully licensed, almost to the day… the rain came and the bottom fell out. Polygraph examiners like myself who caught and failed so many industrial thieves and criminals from the work place in employer-employee relationships were now out in the cold due to changes in the law. Now for the greater part, we were prevented by federal law from protecting employers from internal theft by their employees. This law in turn opened the gates of hell for the employer and every type of deviant employee would rise to the occasion and load up on the assets of their employer.

One particular liberal U.S. Senator on the east coast always comes to mind, a Massachusetts senator, a momma's boy and a fall down drunken stumblebum punk who did everything within his power to destroy our business to only later be exonerated of rape charges by a polygraph examination. The irony of it all overwhelms me at times. The polygraph industry lost approximately 90% of its business in a blink of an eye.

Because of this liberalism, many a businessman was left defenseless to the schemes and scams of their employees who moved through their business assets like swarms of African locusts devouring everything in sight. The employers would call us while on the verge of crying and scream to us for assistance in hopes of saving their business and lifework from vanishing.

But like dying men on the battlefield in no mans land, you could hear their screams and feel their agony but could do little to nothing but weep for them. The rest was history.

Ed`s phone rang.

"Luna Pier Polygraph Service and…."

"Frank, is that you?"

"Whose this, Denise?"

"Yes, you got a moment. I need your viewpoint on the "bomber" case that I'm handling right now, in Ohio. Due to your expertise in bomb training I need you to shed some light on my case."

"Okay, Denise, what you got?"

"Can we talk it over lunch, Frank, I'll buy."

"(Laughing)…A classy gal like you, buying lunch. My, my, I don't think I can let an opportunity like this pass me by. How about Dave's Coney Island?"

"Fine, in about a half hour, Frank."

"I'm on it, Denise."

As I left the office, walking down Main Street to Dave's Coney Island, a five-minute walk, I was thinking about Denise. A real well preserved tall and healthy good-looking doll. But after she went through two bad marriages she never expressed an interest in dating or getting serious again. Too bad, a classy gal like her, honest as they come and the hardest working investigator I have ever seen. In every case, she was a fine interrogator, real proper, thorough and did everything by the numbers.

At Dave's, Denise and I sat in the back by the corner window overlooking the wealthy and upscale people shopping the avenue by Luna Pier. Back in the corner we could discuss privileged information without the concern of snoops and prying eyes overhearing or seeing us.

Dave, the owner, would drop by from time to time and talk about the ponies racing out of Bolles Harbor. I didn't have the heart to tell him that some of the riders that I polygraphed had tipped me off about some of those races weeks in advance. They told me on which horses from which owners to bet on. If I was a gambler, Dave, I could have made a decent chunk of change for the rider's predictions were right seven out of ten times.

Denise and I ordered chilidogs smothered in onions with a side order of greasy fries and cola.

"How was your vacation Frank?"

"To the chase, Denise, good, I went out west and took in the sights, did some amateur geology work on the Little Big Horn mountain range in Wyoming. You know some of those rocks go back about 3.5 billion years, I found that interesting. Then while there and not paying attention to the changing weather I got caught in a severe ice storm at 10,000 feet near Bald Mountain. Not a soul was up there and I almost drove off the road into a deep ravine and entered glory. I thought I would have to scuttle the van and walk off the mountain but within the hour the storm passed and everything was fine. I then went exploring throughout the Redwood Forests in northern California, near Crescent City, god it was beautiful there. Then I had some business to attend to, where I talked to a couple of business executives who wanted investigations on some associates of theirs.

"Sounds like you had a nice time, Frank."

"Trips out west always air out my head and my brain resynchronizes. I find it healthy. What's up with you, Denise?"

"Well, I got this crazy case where a young lady, if I can call her that, is doing time in Toledo, Ohio at Oregon Federal Prison for Women. She received a life sentence for blowing up her husband with a pipe bomb and killing him. She claims she didn't do it and her attorney is trying to get a retrial, though the Court of Appeals denied her. Currently the case is before Ohio's Supreme Court."

"Oh, what's her alibi, Denise?"

"Again, Frank, during my interview she claimed she didn't know how to make a bomb. Are pipe bombs hard to make?"

"No, pipe bombs are not hard to make at all, Denise. But they are one of the most dangerous Improvised Explosive Devices, known as I.E.D.'s, and are very unstable."

Denise looking back from the window, "Why are they dangerous?"

As I signaled for the waitress to return and inform her that the mustard container was empty, "Their dangerous Denise because as the end caps are being secured, more often then not, there is gunpowder residue on the threads of the end cap. When the caps are being tightened down on metal-to-metal, a spark can be generated and the pipe bomb becomes a nasty fragmentation grenade in your hands. Consequently, this usually kills or severely maims the bomber. Another issue to be concerned about is static electricity generated from the synthetic clothes you're wearing which can create a spark and be extremely dangerous."

"Do women make these kinds of devices in your experience, Frank?"

"No, hell no, Denise. Obviously, they have the intelligence to make them, but in my experience they do not make them.

Matter of fact, during the nine years that I have been in the field, both military and civilian and excluding nations at war, I never heard of a woman making an explosive device or a pipe bomb. On the surface, it is my opinion that there's another player in the game, plain and simple!"

"That's what I figured, Frank, it just doesn't add up."

"No it doesn't, Denise. Is this some lover's triangle or what?"

"It appears so, Frank."

"Well, Ed placed me in charge again Denise, so that gives me the option to roam freely in all the company caseloads for the next couple weeks.

Ahh…. tell you what; if you want me to assist in the interrogation, I'll help you as soon as I'm done with my homicide case tomorrow."

"Sounds good Frank, I like to stay on top of the game in this business."

"If you can, Denise, why don't you interview her again and see what further information you can extract. If she claims she didn't do it or doesn't know how to make a pipe bomb then what's her theory as to why she is doing life in prison for murder?"

"She doesn't know who did it, Frank, so she says, but thinks her boyfriend may have done it."

"Oh, the web of deceit one does weave, Denise. Her boyfriend kills her husband then loses his love to a life prison sentence …makes a lot of sense. There has to be more to this."

"Okay, Frank, I'm out of here."

As I made my way home to prepare for tomorrows examination, my body was already itching from the thought of some of these jailhouses. I swear I end up with body lice and bedbugs every time I enter into one of these facilities. It reminds me of one time early in my police career when I was first an ambulance driver and fireman. We got dispatched to a sick lady who lived at the top of a two-story family flat. The stairwell was almost vertical with about twenty steps from the front porch to the upper apartment door. We had to kick in the door because the lady couldn't move and what we found laying there was a 300-pound plus woman who needed medical assistance. She had sores and flaky skin falling off her body, not a good sight before dinner. My partner and I lifted her up and placed her on the stretcher nearly breaking both our backs.

Now, at that time, I knew one of us had to be on the bottom position going down this steep stairwell and one of us had to be on the top position. Unfortunately, I was the one with less seniority; so my partner stated I had to take the bottom position as we went down the stairwell. As soon as we started down the stairwell this lady with her scaly skin disease shifted and slid my way resting on my hands. All her weight now was on my two arms while my deviant partner chuckled. As we went down the steps I pulled every muscle in my back and arms trying to keep this beached whale from falling onto the stairwell. At the brink of collapse, my handgrip started to give and then three of my fingers and my thumbs from both hands gave out. When we got to the ambulance and beached her, I was holding her up with one finger from both hands.

You know, they say people under extreme circumstances can do unbelievable things. Indeed. After we got back to the firehouse both my partner and I got naked and immersed ourselves in fifty-five gallon drums of soap to funk be gone ourselves. Funny how memories resurface…memories of some things the working man must do just to eat.

The next day, I responded over to Cain County Jail and stood in a mile long line to be wand and metal detected along with the dregs of society. Finally a jailer called out, "Any cops present that are needed for legal or administration purposes?" I immediately flipped my badge and was brought through the line like a knife through butter. Reaching the jail administrators front desk, I identified myself and stated my purpose. The jailer queried me about having any guns on my person. I stated, "No, I'm only carrying polygraph equipment." After a brief frisk and equipment search I was allowed to enter the jail proper and taken via elevator to the fourth floor where the inmates were held for murder. I asked the police sheriff who accompanied me if I would be allowed to run the test in a private room to preserve attorney client privilege. He stated, "No", and that I would have to run it in a 4-foot by 8-foot jail cell with the prisoner charged with murder in the first degree for three hours, while he stood down the hall.

I laughed, when the sheriff stated there was no bathroom or water for me except what was in the prisoners abode. Still laughing, I said, "Nothing like accommodations." There are bugs on the wall, the temperature is near 90 degrees, I have no water, no bathroom and I'm in a cell with a murder one suspect for three hours. Life is good. As I entered the jail, I introduced myself to Tyrone, a 19-year-old black male, 6`4' and 250 pounds.

"Tyrone, I want to advise you that I am, Frank Legion, here on behalf of your attorney, Attorney Smith, and that he stated that you are maintaining your innocence that you shot Reggie in self-defense. Is that right?"

"Dats right, Mr. Legion."

"Okay Tyrone, before I start the polygraph examination, I want to advise you that in order for you to pass your polygraph examination you have to tell the truth, the whole truth and nothing but the truth to everything I ask. If you lie to me about anything, anything at all, you fail. Is that understood?"

Tyrone, lying on his bed rack against the orange walls started scratching the chip paint from his bedpost, stated, "Yah."

"Now, Tyrone, I'm going to waive all these legal papers here because legal council represents you. Are you going to allow me to send all the results of this polygraph examination to your attorney for review?"

"Mr. Legion...Ahh...ah right."

"Then lets begin the polygraph examination, Tyrone. First, I'm going to get some information about you, even though your attorney answered the greater portion already. Again, understand you must answer each question truthfully or you will fail your examination."

Tyrone's rubbing his nose and pulling his ear, "Ahh right."

"Do you work, Tyrone?"

"Whhaa, I'm unemployed, Mr. Legion."

"Tyrone, have you ever been arrested or brought before the judge for anything?"

"Yah, ahh.... for disorderly and a cocaine charge two-years ago that didn't stick and dis felony murder charge."

"That's a lot of stuff, Tyrone, for a 19-year-old black male. What can you say about yourself?"

"Ahh...I'm a nice guy, Mr. Legion. Yes, ah iz."

"Have you ever been falsely accused of anything you did not do, Tyrone?"

"Yah, ...a cocaine rap two years ago."

"Is that all, Tyrone?"

"Yah, dats right Mr. Legion."

"Tyrone, why do you want to take a polygraph examination?

Tyrone responded, "Ahh, want to show dat, I'm telling da truth and dat the statement the witness said was not true."

I then asked, "What was the witnesses name, Tyrone? Male...female? Black.... white...age?"

Tyrone replied as he stared at an old knife wound on his arm, " Miss Carter is a black-female about 40 years old."

"Tyrone, what is Miss Carter stating that concerns you?"

"Miss Carter claims, Mr. Legion, she seen me in da car with Reggie just before he got killed."

"Tyrone, the case facts show that this incident happened November 2, 2009, on Spruce Street, Oregon, Ohio, around 8:45 p.m. near the Rainbow Bridge. Further, Reggie was shot in the head and chest multiple times. Are those facts correct?"

"Ahh…yes…ah guess, Mr. Legion."

"Tyrone, do you know who shot Reggie?  Who may have helped to shoot him?  Have you heard any word on the street who wanted to shoot him?"

"No…Mr. Legion, I've been thinking seriously about dis polygraph…. can I say som'n?  I want to level with you, and just asken, if I told you the truth to what really happened, will I pass my test?"

"Tyrone, my brother, if you answer truthfully to all my questions you will pass your examination with flying colors.  Understand, confession to committing a crime or admitting to elements of the crime is a polygraph examination.  The only way your situation can be improved is for you to tell me the truth so your attorney can better represent you and perhaps plea bargain on your behalf.  Are you going to tell me the whole truth?  Otherwise, you rot here.  I don't care either way, I made a grand on this case already and tonight I'm going home and having a beer."

"Hmmm…ahh...right, Mr. Legion.  It went like this, ya understand.  Reggie took me for a ride to discuss some prior business.  Reggie was mad at me for not paying him $500 dollars I owed him recently and another $1,000 dollars that I owed him for some crack I sold.  Reggie was a wild man and I was scared of him."

"Okay, I'm listening, Tyrone."

"As we went down under the Rainbow Bridge, I thought Reggie was going to beat the shit out of me.  So, I pulled out my .22 automatic pistol from beneath my belt that I carry for self-defense and shot him in the head and chest.  He den fell out of da car."

"Tyrone, are you saying to me you shot Reggie in cold blood with your own pistol without any provocation from him?"

"Yah…as Reggie fell out of the car, he was still moving and staggering around by da car.  When da car finally stopped rolling, ah jumped out and ran back around to the drivers side to finish off Reggie and shot him again in da chest and head."

"Okay Tyrone, did Reggie ever show you a gun, threaten you with a gun or attempt to shoot you with a gun?"

"No! I just shot him because I thought he was going to "whip my ass" for not paying him da money.  I thought he was going to "do me in" so I shot him first."

"Tyrone, why did you not inform your attorney of the true circumstances surrounding this case?"

"If my attorney knew da truth as I just told you, he would not represent me and I would have to "push time for murder in prison." I don't want you to tell my attorney now. Ah.... Ah, I didn't mean to kill him."

"Tyrone, I have been assigned here on behalf of the judge and your attorney. I will have to forward this privileged information to your attorney so you can be properly defended for murder in the first degree? Your attorney has requested that I ask you specific questions:

(1) Did the victim pull a handgun on you in the car?

Your testimony was "No."

(2) Did you struggle with Reggie over a gun?

You answered "No." Then you stated you just shot Reggie in cold blood.

(3) Was Reggie shot accidentally while the two of you were struggling with a gun?

Again, your answer was "No."

"Ahh, Mr. Legion... ah know it was wrong for me to fabricate this story and withhold facts from my attorney."

"Damn right.... imagine if you said this before a jury and judge.... your finished. The only hope you have now Tyrone is that your attorney can possibly work out a plea bargain with the information I provide him.

Okay, back at the scene when you shot Reggie in the head and chest the second time did he die?"

"No, sir. He fell under da car. Then I ran back to da car, jumped in and tried to drive away."

"Okay Tyrone, continue."

"Den.... I drove over Reggie with the car as I tried to get away."

"Tyrone, are you serious or are you lying to me?"

"I'm serious, mister, I told you the man wanted to beat the shit outta me, so it was me or him. I then backed up over him again and again."

"Why didn't you just leave, Tyrone, Reggie must have been dead by then?"

"I was not sure he was dead, Mr. Legion, so I just kept driving over him?"

"Tyrone, what made you finally decide to leave the area in the vehicle?"

"I didn't leave in da vehicle, mister."

"Explain why not, Tyrone.... I mean I'm all ears?"

"Because the wheels wouldn't turn, mister."

"What do you mean the wheels wouldn't turn, Tyrone, you just said you ran over him numerous times?"

"Mr. Legion, Reggie's whole body was stuck up in da wheel well and the wheels wouldn't turn...so I jumped out of da car and ran."

"Tyrone, did I hear you right... that Reggie's whole body was stuck up in the wheel well?

"Yah, that's what I'm saying, Mr. Legion. It was self-defense."

"So you left Reggie's body stuffed up in the vehicle's wheel well and just like that you suddenly just walked out of his life? Is that right, Tyrone?"

Tyrone rubbing his nose and scratching the chip paint from beneath his finger nails, stated, "Yah."

"It is a good thing you're telling me this instead of to a jury, Tyrone. I do believe your attorney is going to pass out when he reads my report."

"Did I pass, Mr. Legion?"

"Yes, Tyrone, you passed your polygraph examination by confessing to murder one. Yes, you passed, my brother. Due to the severity of your crime though, I'm going to polygraph you anyway in regards to your confession to ensure it is truthful."

"Ahh right...my man, Mister Legion."

After verifying, Tyrone's confession that he told the truth to murdering Reggie, I advised Tyrone that he had passed his polygraph examination to committing murder one. When I looked at Tyrone's face after I told him he passed he looked downright righteous as if he had gone to glory.

"Tyrone, your attorney will get my report tomorrow and he will confide with you regarding your charge and confession to murder one. Tyrone, this time tell your attorney the whole truth."

I looked at the jail cell door and called out, "Sheriff, can I get out of here."

The Sheriff looked at me and stated, "Damn, ninety minutes that was fast. How did he do?"

As I looked at the sheriff laughing, I stated, "As you most probably overheard, he's done like dinner, Sheriff. You and me both know that some people are made for prison. Tyrone is one of them. As the saying goes, "you can't cure dumb.""

Returning to Luna Pier, I couldn't help but admire the wisdom and foresight of Ed buying these investigative buildings for polygraphs and private investigations on beachfronts with a fishing pier. Luna Pier with its windswept shoreline sure beat the inner city blight and clientele. Many a day I would spend my time smoking Robusto cigars with Ed while sitting out on that thousand-foot pier. Myself and other associates would discuss criminal cases late into the night especially if someone bought a six-pack of beer.

The sounds of the great lake freighters, the fishermen and the laughter of children playing in the surf of Lake Erie were delightful. I found the view from the pier to be gorgeous, refreshing and therapeutic after a long days work.

## *Chapter 2 - Till death do us part*

After a day of report writing, I handed Attorney Smith's report on Tyrone for Murder One to Coco for processing. While I was walking away, Coco began reading my report and before I could hit the coffee pot, I heard her yell out, "Oh my God!"

"What's the matter Coco, too hot in the kitchen?" I replied, "Too grisly?"

"Thank God, Tyrone's in prison." Coco replied back.

"Indeed Coco, he was born for prison."

While I was waiting for Denise to respond back from Ohio, to review her case, I pondered over the caseload of the ten Luna Pier investigators who were dispatched all over God's creation. As I reflected over their specific caseload to determine how best to handle them, Coco called over the intercom, "You have a call Frank from an Attorney Ron, from Indiana."

"Oh? Okay on the Attorney Ron, Coco."

As I picked up the phone, I stated, "Yes sir, how can I help you?"

Through the crackling sounds of a bad telephone connection, I could hear a voice say, "Mr. Legion, how are you?"

"I'm fine sir, thank you and yourself?"

"Fine, thank you. Mr. Legion, I am from a large firm and I wanted to know if you could run some well established clients of mine who are in need of a polygraph examination."

"Sure why not. Sir, I didn't get your full name?"

"Well, I'm an attorney and if I may, Mr. Ron will do for now."

"Okay," I stated, "You want to remain anonymous counselor? Caller I.D. states out of area. Have we done work for you in the past?"

"Well, Mr. Legion, I'm calling from Indiana. Yes, I would like to remain anonymous for now. No, I have not had any polygraph work or investigative work assigned to your firm before. The examiner I was using for years, in which I had an excellent relationship with, was a retired federal agent from Indiana who recently died from heart complications. However, since his death I have been in need of a licensed and certified polygraph examiner to help my clients."

"Okay," I stated, as I mentally stepped back awaiting his opening move.

"My question is Mr. Legion, if I went with your firm would you be able to help my clients and pass them. Again, my clients are well established and most of them are charged with allegations of white-collar crime and dealings with the underworld. I have sufficient amount of clients and I want to ensure that they will be given the best deal possible."

As red flags began to go up in my head, I hoped that I misunderstood Mr. Ron, by reading between the lines, "Best deal? Pass them? What does that mean Mr. Ron?"

"Well, will you pass my clients, Mr. Legion, if I bring them to you? It would be a significant amount of revenue for your firm and I would like to establish the same relationship I had with my former polygraph examiner."

Now knowing where this conversation was going I stated, "Mr. Ron, the only way your clients are going to pass with this firm or with me is if they tell the truth. If you're asking me to tilt the scale in favor of your clients, Mr. Ron, then you have come to the wrong firm. To cut to the chase, your clients have to tell the truth to all the questions I ask them or they fail outright. Do we have an understanding on this Mr. Ron before we proceed forward, or should you hang up on me now?"

"Well, Mr. Legion, you are going to lose a lot of business from my firm unless you cooperate."

"Mr. Ron, in this polygraph profession, business attorneys quickly find out that they do not talk down to polygraph examiners, nor do they tell us what to do. If by chance an attorney doesn't know that, then they will quickly find out that they don't have a polygraph examiner. This firm's polygraph examiners have integrity and we are not street pimps nor hustlers, nor do we sell our soul to the devil. Regarding losing your business I guess that's why I've been working all my life. It's called an honest days work.

Moreover, I'm well aware of the polygraph examiner who worked for you. As professional licensed investigators we have our own grapevine and channels of information not accessible to the ordinary man on the street, including you sir.

That federal polygraph examiner that you are implying about from that three-letter agency that you hired from had apparently gone rogue. Just so you know, before this polygraph examiner in question died, an attorney requested that the examiner run a polygraph examination on a sheriff who raped a woman in Indiana and it was front-page news nationwide."

Mr. Ron, (clears throat).

"Counselor, this may come as a surprise to you, but before your friend the federal examiner took the case, I already had been presented with the case and turned it down. Due to this, I had an extreme interest in this case since good publicity for polygraph examiners on the front-page of a nationwide newspaper would be fantastic for business.

However, when I told the attorney in question that I would do my best to obtain justice for his client using the polygraph technique, he hesitated. I further stated his client must understand that his only obligation is to tell the truth. After further conversation, the attorney decided not to go with me because he felt I would fail his client if he lied. Well, your friend, the federal examiner, took the case, got the money and passed the sheriff on rape charges. There was great jubilation needless to say from the sheriff's "intimate circle" that enjoyed celebrity status while I sat there empty handed without the business or the fame.

But then fate took a strange twist as it often does, for the same three letter federal agency your friend formerly worked for and trained under refused to accept his results. They refused their own examiner's results who they trained, strange isn't it?

Further, this was stated on the front page of various newspapers and editorial sections, which brought the polygraph technique in question. I found this highly unusual and wondered why a federal agency like that would do this to one of their own credible and long-standing polygraph examiners?

At this time I received information regarding your polygraph friend from an associate of mine, who was also a seasoned polygraph examiner and a police detective as well. He informed me that your polygraph friend, who worked in the private sector, had passed a questionable subject in regards to a high profile case for the defense and now he; the police detective, would be examining the same subject in the public sector and for the prosecuting attorney.

Furthermore, your polygraph friend tried to influence the police detective's polygraph examination by having him also compromise his integrity. However, the police detective refused to taint the examination and failed the examinee on the case facts presented. The detective in turn told your examiner friend that he was "throwing tests" for money and that he would be no part of that.

The fact is counselor, that it was common knowledge in the polygraph field especially among us street examiners that your friend appeared to put his "thumb on the scale" in favor of the highest bidder.

In the end "your friend" who sold out for "Judas money" cost him his life.

Then your friend's former employer, the three-letter agency, who refused your friends results decided also to reach their own findings and they did, they failed the sheriff.

As I'm sure you know, the Indiana Sheriff is doing time for rape and your polygraph friend has died suddenly and unexpectedly. Which was probably due, in part, to the embarrassment and stress of people learning of his corruption. Now, the people who paid him good money and the sheriff's "inner circle" were asking themselves now, how could this be?

So in reality, I won in the end by losing the money, whereas your friend may have made the money but lost his life in the process. So the moral of the story is this, if justice cannot be served then let the heavens fall.

So my question to you Mr. Ron, is this, were you the attorney who called me that one sunny day and refused me because I wouldn't sell out? If so, how's your conscience now or does it matter?"

"Mr. Legion, you're reaching and obviously in need of medical attention, I see no reason to continue this conversation or do business with you."

"By the way, Mr. Ron, what if I told you this conversation is taped and what if I forwarded this tape to the state licensing board…(click)…. Hello, hello.. Mr. Ron are you there?"

As I put down the phone, I could not help but wonder about the audacity and arrogance of some polygraph examiners and attorneys. How so many are book smart but street stupid. How can some examiners cave in just for the temptation of money? I mean we all need the money but if we are the salt of the earth and have lost our taste then what good are we?

Like myself, each examiner in the State of Michigan must have a college degree or higher. The work as an intern is very hard and for four years you work for nothing by doing two hundred criminal specific examinations at various locations on your own time.

Each case's duration takes from ninety minutes to four hours in order to get those "two hundred dit`s" to help you qualify to take a four hour state license examination.

I couldn't help but wonder why an examiner would destroy their reputation and integrity just for a few thousand dollars. It escapes me how some examiners after years of internship work, state exams and oral boards who finally become a state licensed polygraph examiner would throw tests. Moreover, by throwing tests they ultimately lose their livelihood; lose their public and private polygraph-investigators license. Then worst of all, they who were placed in a position of trust lose their integrity, respect and as in this particular case, their life.

It's astounding how a person can throw away their life's work of healing the injustices against humanity by prostituting themselves to some creeping crud attorney and his underworld figures for blood money.

As I walked to the window fuming from this last conversation, I slowly calmed down as I looked out across Lake Erie watching the Great Lake freighters crossing in front of Ohio's Davis-Besse nuclear power plant. I couldn't help but wonder how the investigative firms across the lake at our sister offices in Maumee Bay, Ohio and the Toledo Light House were doing and if their caseload were as hectic as ours.

"Frank."

"Oh…. hi Denise, I didn't see you come in. Must have been daydreaming. What's going on with your case?"

"Well, Frank, this case is getting crazier and crazier. After I talked with Rosemary, the examinee, she again stated she drove her vehicle from Lansing, Michigan to Toledo, Ohio and parked the car in her driveway on Spruce Street. She then proceeds to enter her house for whatever reason. The car is left in the driveway until the following day when her husband comes out of their house to start the car and the seat he is sitting on explodes killing him instantly."

"That's insane, Denise. Rosemary is doing life for making an explosive device, which killed her husband? Yet, I'm to believe that she drove a car ninety miles to her home with an unstable pipe bomb that she placed beneath her driver's seat, that she made. This is tantamount to having a bottle of nitro-glycerin beneath you and yet I'm to believe she drove this car with an armed explosive device while listening to the radio and checking out her mascara in the rear view mirror. It escapes me that if a person had the know how to make such an explosive device like she allegedly did, then who but a brain dead moron would want to sit on top of it? From what you just told me, Denise, that doesn't make sense at all. Moreover, what was she doing in Lansing?"

As Denise was trying to make sense of it all she stated, "She told her husband she took the car up there to have the muffler fixed by a friend, if you can believe that?"

"What are you saying, Denise? There are muffler shops on every other block on any main drag and I'm suppose to believe she had to drive ninety miles to find a muffler shop? Bullshit! I can't believe it. She didn't do it or her story is seriously flawed, plain and simple."

"Frank, she was found convicted for killing her husband. It was a trial by jury and they believed she made the bomb and sentenced her to life imprisonment. She has been serving time for eight years and is hoping to get a retrial. The appellate court denied her a retrial and her case is up before the Ohio Supreme Court. Her husband, Mumdu, was cut in two from the explosion.

Funny though, an Alcohol, Tobacco and Firearm expert, who was also trained in explosives testified at the trial and he reached the same conclusion you did that Rosemary didn't make the device."

"A.T.F. are good people, Denise, among the best bomb technicians in the country, as a matter-of-fact.

However, you would think that the jury would have given more weight and credibility to the agents' testimony. I'm not surprised that the A.T.F. agent and myself both coming from two different paths arrived independently at the same conclusion and we further appear to be reading from the same sheet of music. To the chase, Rosemary didn't do it. I believe we can prove it because we have another weapon in our arsenal that the A.T.F. agent did not have at the time. That weapon of choice is the polygraph instrument which will allow us to penetrate deeper into this web of deceit or truth by applying the polygraph technique."

"Her court attorney, Frank, is "Buck" Travis, a big gun attorney who is handling the case. He also believes his client, has been set up."

"I agree, Denise. What's the status on her boyfriend anyway? We got anything?"

"Apparently Frank, he works in a car shop and goes by the nickname, "Trooper." Outside of that, Rosemary, the alleged bomber, will not shed any more light on him."

"Denise, why the hell should she protect him? She's been in jail eight years and is doing life, what has she got to lose by dropping a dime on him?"

Denise jumped back, "I don't know why she is protecting him, perhaps she's in love with him. Perhaps he has something over on her or maybe he is innocent."

"What does that mean, Denise? Are we looking into a love triangle scenario or are we getting into a conspiracy now?"

"I don't know at this moment, Frank. But, I do know Rosemary and Mumdu were having monetary problems besides marital problems."

"A lot of marriages have money and marital problems, but I don't find that sufficient to blow up your spouse in two.

But, then I guess I'm talking to the choir on this one, Denise."

"Yes, you are. The sword cuts both ways Frank. My men had drinking, gambling and women problems, not a safe environment for children."

"I'm sorry Denise, I was out of line."

"How about you Frank? Its been two years now, are you still in mourning?"

" .........Yes, still...still. Denise, when you going to test Rosemary?"

"Well, I got clearance from the jail administrator, Frank, to run the exam tomorrow at 9 a.m. or the following day at 11 a.m. I would rather go tomorrow at 9 a.m. if that's okay with you?"

"That will work, Denise. Good, 9 a.m. is fine for tomorrow, I will meet you here at 8 a.m. and we'll take the company car down."

"Fine, I will see you then Frank and we can discuss the case further. I'm going to call the attorney now and see if everything is still good to go. Then I'm heading home to finish up some loose ends."

"Okay, Denise. I'll be talking to you."

After Denise left, I walked out on the pier and couldn't help but admire, the beautiful blue sky and the tranquil sound of the waves hitting the dock. As I sat there on a bench, I lit up a nice mild smoking Robusto cigar and took in the sights. Down the beach, I could see the attractive and well-to-do ladies strutting around in front of their cottages without a care in the world. It's got to be nice, but where's the men, I wondered?

As I was walking my way back from the 1,000-foot pier to the office, Coco called out.

"Frank, Solar, from the Solar Process Server and Investigation Service wants to talk to you and please Frank, leave the cigar outside."

Laughing, "Is it the smell, Coco, or did you quit smoking?"

"I don't smoke and cigars stink, Frank."

"I'll make a mental note of that Coco."

Picking up the phone, "Solar, what's up?"

"Frank, thank God, I got you. I need your help big time on this one my man."

"I'm listening, Solar."

"Frank, I got a gentleman who has had an affair. His wife suspects he is running around and she is going to divorce him if he doesn't level with her. He needs a polygraph examination Frank to clear himself."

"We can do that, Solar."

"Ahh…Frank, he needs a favor and needs to pass his polygraph examination to save his marriage."

"Solar, it must be a full moon today. Tell him this; all he has to do to pass his examination is to tell the truth that he is not whoring around on his wife. That's simple enough, isn't it?"

"Frank, he is willing to pay $10,000 dollars, if you help him."

"Solar, polygraph examinations don't come in different flavors, you know that. Why are you doing this to me? We have done a lot of legitimate business in the past, okay. Why are you bringing this garbage to my doorstep? You already know the answer. Tell the crack head, no."

"Ahh…He is not a crack head Frank, he is the husband of a high-ranking politician."

"Oh boy, here we go, how high, Solar?"

"Governor! Frank, he is willing to go as high as $15,000. I'd appreciate it if you reconsider and help me out here, Frank."

"Wow, Solar, in less then a minute the polygraph examination has gone up $5,000 dollars. That's good money for one examination.

But guess what, I know who that hustler is. He may have won a couple million-dollar contracts, Solar, without legally bidding for them at the Mattawan International Airport, but we both know that his pixie wife, the governess, covered him.

Furthermore, despite his political connection he'll get no favor here and the answer is still no. One more thing, if you bring another case of this nature to my door-step again Solar, I'm going to inform Ed and the state licensing board on you."

Solar yelled, "I'm just trying to make you some money, Frank."

"Thanks for looking out for me Solar, it was nice talking to you, goodbye."

Thinking to myself, I wondered how could some people run a business like they do. I mean where is their conscience. Yet, as outward appearances go, life has shown me that the cheater has received far more good breaks in life then what the honest man receives. At times I swear I don't belong on this planet anymore. The world appears to have changed in so many ways for the worst despite advancement in technology.

I couldn't help but ponder how obvious it had become to see people without a moral compass. The direction in which people have changed can be observed through noticeable subtle indicators such as their order of importance in the holiday seasons for days such as Halloween, Thanksgiving and Christmas.

Though I know my theory is not conclusive, per se, nevertheless, I have noticed a metamorphosis, a transformation, of human society that has occurred within the last twenty years. A rather significant change as a matter of fact, yet mostly undetected by the untrained eye. What I mean is, people for the greater part today are too busy looking at their day to day affairs, as in money, while totally overlooking subtle details of the encroachment of evil that will render their life's work on earth useless.

People understand the signs of the weather, as in, "Red sky at night, sailors delight" or, "Red sky at morning sailors take warning." Yet the signs of the times of imminent encroaching evil they either can't see it or they refuse to admit what they see."

Halloween, in time past, started the holiday's season in which children would come out with their innocence during the children's hour, which was the hour between the dusk and the darkness. The streets were full of thousands of laughing children, who moved like army ants throughout the neighborhood. Every single resident homeowner gave delicious treats to the children on their day of enchantment. For the cities, villages and the public square knew that the children were their future and their hope.

In those days, the kids would return home after a long night of trick or treating and dump out two, three or even four large grocery bags of candy on the kitchen table.

This was the Halloween, I vividly remember.

Thanksgiving, the second festive calendar occasion, was a time where people appreciated a stuffed baked turkey with all of the trimmings. It was a very memorable event because family and friends would gather together for the celebration to give praise to the God of heaven and drink the wine of the earth.

Talk of the hunting season among men was always in the air at the dinner table while the women and children talked about which float at the Thanksgiving Day parade was the best.

Thanksgiving, in those days was a preconditioning for people to raise their consciousness that a great and joyous celebration of Christmas was about to occur in a month.

The holiday season of Christmas, as I remembered, was the most festive celebration of the three holidays. People would go to a great extent to decorate their houses with lovely ornaments that lit up the dreary nights of winter.

Further, there was a sense of goodwill to men and Santa really did exist. There were snowball fights everywhere and kids laughing while hitching rides behind cars in lighted snow-covered streets. None of us kids had money, yet our hearts and stomachs were full. There were parties on every block and people would invite you into their homes just for the sole purpose of casual conversation and offer you food and drink.

Women looked and dressed like women then and men looked, dressed and acted like gentlemen. Everyone went to church and paid homage to the God of heaven, in those days.

Today, the spirit of Christmas has changed; a sense of paganism has taken over. You can feel it all around you, you can smell it in the air, for men do not fear God or respect or believe in his presence anymore.

Accordingly, it reflects in their actions and conduct especially towards their treatment of women and towards their fellow man. Marriage is not a sacred oath, "until death do us part," but rather a shack up job until something better comes along.

Women are not perceived as a gift from God anymore but rather a thing, a seed bank or a shank of meat. Women are not looked upon as prospectus mothers anymore. Nor are they seen in their truest of forms as an organic star gate that is the recipient of souls to obtain form. Today women are perceived as an innate object, soulless, like salt of the earth, which has lost its flavor.

Today men have become Godless an obvious indicator, though perceived as a harmless cultural statement, is when they cover their whole body with desecrating tattoos that defile them. This desecration is a reflection of an immerging dark inner soul from within and a preference for a criminal disposition.

In the past the only people who covered their whole body with tattoos were criminals from the penal system, harpoon whale hunters and the circus men who swept up elephant pies at the end of a parade.

Today, tattoos are a statement of gang mentality that has given way to a lower order of recessive and devolving humans where the rule of law is based solely upon "might makes right." The tattoos as they are used today are a desecrating mark, an indicator and a preconditioning to the acceptance of the mark of the beast.

This spiritual change to welcoming the encroaching darkness with open arms has reared its destructive nature throughout my thirty years in the streets as a polygraph examiner. I have for thirty years entered and witnessed numerous broken homes with screaming mothers, who have caught venereal diseases from their husbands who have denied an extraneous affair and watched when their wives pulled guns on them when they failed their tests.

I have found women on the floor beaten and unconscious just because their husband suspected that a blurred photo of an unknown female giving oral sex in a porn magazine was their wife.

I have seen women put scissors in their police husband's chest and those who wanted their husbands tested for infidelity yet tell me on the side that if their husband fails they will kill themselves…*in front of me* because they could not handle the truth.

I have seen men beg me to run further polygraph examinations on their wives to say "it isn't so Joe" after their wives had confessed to me that they had extramarital affairs with 10 or more men since they been married.

The screaming of well-to-do beautiful women who have contracted venereal diseases from their husbands, who in turn twist the facts and blame their wives.

I have witnessed the total destruction and implosion of the family structure first-hand that exists from the wealthiest to the street people at an exponential speed.

It is my belief that mothers who are breast feeding today shall not see fruition for their labors, for a child born now is tantamount to planting a young sprouting tomato plant in Michigan in the middle of December…*vanities of vanity, all is vanity.*

The suicidal tendency of so many fathers falsely accused by their senseless daughters and stepdaughters today is heartbreaking. The daughters and especially stepdaughters extort their own fathers and stepfathers by accusing them, *in court*, that they were molested in order to get back at their father for not giving them their way on a particular issue.

I stood crushed and broken when I witnessed innocent workingmen being arrested and sent to prison on fabricated charges because their passed polygraph examinations were declared inadmissible.

Before me stands broken families in a state of total chaos and without hope as mothers weep and children go forth without protection.

The endless faces of terrified children who looked at me with fear in their eyes who knew intuitively that something horrible is transpiring before them, defenseless and helpless they are, their tomorrow now uncertain.

*If I don't help them, then who will? Surely not the broken legal system, which enslaves the innocent and frees the guilty? A carousel of laws that is at best a travesty of justice that places heavy burdens upon men.*

*What stands before me is not the word of the law, but the spirit of the law...free these captive souls, so they may know justice and live!*

*Or let the heavens fall!*

*I have to save as many of these innocent mothers and fathers and their children as I can!*

*I have to at all cost...yes, at all cost!*

*They must have hope, they must!*

*I go in alone with notched gun for my work is not for the weak of heart. Yet, I know out there my final destiny is inevitable, for I have a rendezvous with death.*

*This is how I feed my family; this is how I keep my family from want, destitute and the harsh realities of life.*

Today, there is little household décor for Thanksgiving, the least of the three celebrated holidays. The detail for cooking a turkey is looked upon as a nuisance and most people could care less to give thanks for their blessings or bounty.

There is no prayer at the table to praise the God of glory for their blessings anymore. Their plates are full yet their soul is empty.

Men have become godless today for they do not believe in anything but themselves, for as it was in the days of Noah so shall it be at the end of this age.

This spiritual mentality and health of my people, the Americans, can ultimately be seen today through the reflection of today's Halloween. Halloween was primarily in days gone by, an effort to laugh at the pagan harvest and the fears of darkness in the following nights. Today's Halloween is a bigger day of decorations and parties then Christmas which can be seen throughout the neighborhoods where residents go to great lengths and expense to adorn their houses with symbolic forms of darkness. For today's Halloween is not the intended, enchanted or magical hour for children anymore.

No, Halloween today has become the most celebrated event of the three celebrations. For it is the long awaited hour of the occult and the black mass. It is the hour of Satan worshipping, the rise of witches and warlocks who have even enthroned Lucifer in the Vatican with their human and animal sacrifices.

Yes, the time of black magic has come to a once god-fearing people. It is the time for the ascent of the Prince from the abyss who calls his human demons to come forth in their disguised human form, *in masse*.

For they walk in human form as men but are not men. It is the time of desecration, the rise of the sodomites with their recessive genes and demonic mentality and conduct. For the hour of shedding blood of the children and the innocent has come in full force today in our presence, in broad daylight.

*All this brutal destruction of the family is reflected and observed in the polygraph profession.*

Mankind, once the salt of the earth, has metamorphosis into a mutated regressive being. As in the movie, "Charley," mankind is regressing back to a lower order of being without question.

Suddenly, as if I were tasered, I returned from my subconscious thought. As my bearings resynchronized I returned back to this moment in time and space.

"Coco, hold my calls, I'm heading upstairs to check on tomorrows caseload, then home to check on my dog, Scooter."

"Okay, Frank."

The following day after a turbulent night sleep tending to my sick dog, Scooter, I headed off to work and arrived at the office at 8:00 a.m. sharp. Within a minute or two Denise arrived carrying a couple cups of coffee and doughnuts.

Good God, she's pretty, well groomed, tall and leggy with eyes of a cat.

We grabbed a new SUV company car and headed downstream to Oregon Ohio Federal Prison for females. While Southbound on I-75 we had a general conversation and discussion on the various aspects of the case.

"I appreciate you coming Frank, two heads are always better then one. It is my belief that if Rosemary is involved in anyway as in a conspiracy, she's finished."

"Indeed, Denise. She's already finished she's doing life. The only thing that can help her now is if her attorney can get a retrial and hopefully the polygraph examination will be the catalyst. In any case, it's an uphill battle."

"Do you mind if I ask you Frank, whatever got you into explosives?"

"Denise, years ago I would have been upset or angry with you asking me such a question, but now there is so much water under the bridge that the hurt and pain is mostly gone.

I was a commissioned officer in the United States Marine Corps as an aviator in pilot training. I was hoping to make jets and fly F-4 Phantoms off of aircraft carriers during the Vietnam War. In those days it was a patriotic duty to answer the call of your country and it was a boyhood dream of mine to fly. To the quick, I was in the advance pilot training stage with about three days left before getting my wings when I encountered a real S.O.B. flight instructor, who had it out for *certain* student pilots. He deliberately failed three of us students just before we were about to graduate.

The American people spent one million dollars training me, yet despite that, I was not allowed to complain and found it near impossible to challenge and reverse a superior officers decision, as wrong as it was.

Nevertheless, all three of us commissioned officers tried but "the powers that be," which were not diligent in their duties overruled. We were denied full officers mast before the Commandant of the Marine Corps and we were not given the opportunity to state our case or have access to the evidence to prove ourselves.

Later, we found out the S.O.B. flight instructor was trial boarded and taken off of flight status and then kicked out of the Marine Corps. The Marine Corps was too embarrassed to admit they had an unqualified instructor training student pilots in advanced training, and that he deliberately failed those who were not to his liking based on his whims and fancy, but not facts. So they covered up all correspondence and communication regarding the instructor's dismissal while our legitimate complaints filed under the Freedom of Information and Privacy Act were pigeonholed.

Later they offered me an early out in an apparent compensation but I refused it. We were blackballed and railroaded and the Marine Corps covered the instructors' transgression even after realizing we told the truth, yet they wouldn't reinstate us for fear of rocking the boat. I stood before a Marine Corps Colonel who cried, literally cried in front of me, when he found out what happened. Imagine, I joined the Marine Corps to fight and if need be to die for my country when it needed me.

43

I didn't run or become a draft dodger but I answered the call. Yet, in my hour of need and cry for justice they refused me my day in court and the opportunity to stand before my peers and correct the wrong. It was more convenient for them to leave us disgraced and turn a blind eye for the sake of some admiral's pension. I felt so powerless after this and ashamed of what they did when they denied the truth and placed the blame where it suited them.

The American taxpayer paid at least one million dollars to train me to fly and I met the challenge. I was ready to get my wings pinned on my chest when along comes this irresponsible flight instructor with an axe to grind, and who for no apparent reason ultimately destroys the dreams and hopes of three young Marine aviators.

The rest is history, I was sent to Marine Corp Combat Engineer School and learned explosives, of which I like to think I was very good at. While I was there I swore to the heavens above a blood oath that if I ever came across a man or woman who walks this earth and was *falsely accused* I would tenaciously and diligently fight for their cause within the framework of the law and despite their status. *For my mission was simple, free the captive innocent and fail and expose the deceitful at all cost.*

After I fulfilled my military obligation and received my honorable discharge, I continued my explosive training by going to advanced bomb school at Huntsville, Alabama and post blast training at the Federal Law Enforcement Training Command in Glynco, Georgia. Both of these are regarded as the best civilian-law enforcement bomb training schools in the United States.

During that time, I trained with Navy Seals, C.I.A., F.B.I., New York Bomb Squad, Israeli's experts and all branches of military intelligence and civilian personnel. Funny, some bomb technicians were just known as John Doe #1, #2, etc. We were told they were from the National Security Agency or some unknown super secret agency, but who knows. I trained with the best of the best and I learned a lot. The bomb technicians I met were some of the finest American patriots I have ever known second only to the men and women of the Marine Corps. Later, I worked on call for various police agencies as a bomb squad technician for seven years and worked in conjunction with state police units and military ordnance specialists out of Selfridge Air Force Base, Michigan.

"Hopefully, I was brief, but there you have it. Someday, I'll tell you why I got into the polygraph profession, but that is a whole story unto itself."

"Did it ever cross your mind that you could get killed Frank?"

"Yes, hell yes, Denise, it did cross my mind and I almost got killed a couple times. A couple cases come to mind as a matter-of-fact. One time, when I was working the Arab section in Dearborn, Michigan, which is the largest concentration of Arabs in North America, I received a call that an explosive package had arrived at the Dearborn Police station. The Dearborn Police Department called my unit for assistance because all their bomb technicians were out of state. When I arrived at the rear of the station a police cruiser met me with two Dearborn Police officers who handed me a lettered envelope that they received from an Arabic travel agency.

According to the officer's testimony they stated that the travel agency was terrified to open it up because on the stamped envelope was written, "God is great!" and "Death to Israel!" The envelope had handwriting on it that was written in English and Arabic. As the envelope was nonchalantly placed in my hands, I froze upon seeing what was on it. I then told the officers to get me the bomb bucket in order to transport this envelope in question to a safe location. I then placed the letter in the bomb bucket and put on my bomb suit for protection. The envelope was transported to the impound yard at the rear of the station which contained a holding area known as a bomb pit.

At this time, I placed the envelope in question in the pit and I pulled out my pocketknife and sliced open the outer edge of the envelope in order to avoid any pressure on possible contact plates that may be pressure release switches and would detonate upon opening. Finally, I peered inside the envelope and I could see an electronic board with small lights blinking which was hooked up to what appeared to be a small amount of high explosives known as C-4.

Mind you, the envelope is about one inch from my nose. When I saw this I immediately rolled my body over to get my face away from the envelope. As I was lying on my back and looking up into the blue sky, I began thinking about a plan of action when suddenly a police officer came running up to me and stated per the chief of police that the travel agents wanted their envelope back. The police officer then states that the envelope is not to be damaged and forthwith to be brought into the station for some strange reason.

As I'm sitting there pondering the insanity of what's transpiring, out of the blue the F.B.I. calls and tells the chief of police that they want me to disassemble and disarm the explosive device and bring the parts to them without damaging same.

At that moment in time I was mad as hell, so I stormed into the chiefs office where I observed an Arab female travel agent accompanied by the chief with a very concerned expression on her face. I told the chief what I observed in the letter and that I am not moving or giving the letter to anyone.

Moreover, I'm going to blow that letter in place with C-4 and if the F.B.I. wants to dissemble or disarm this explosive device then they can get their paper pushing asses away from their desks and get down here and do it themselves. After the chief heard my story and over the objection of the tourist agent, he ordered me for safety sakes to blow it in place with high explosives."

"Frank, why would the Arab travel agent want the explosive letter back and why would the F.B.I. want you to place yourself at risk like that?"

"Good question Denise, but we have to delve into the realm of conspiracy now and the reality is totally contrary to what the public is being told by our government. *Remember Denise everything I am telling you today and will tell you about explosives and what I know, **is a blatant lie**, I'm lying to you Denise. Do you understand me?"*

"Frank, I get your drift."

"*Remember,* Denise, *that the government version of 9/11 is totally correct and that what I'm about to tell you is speculation, conjecture and that my story is totally incorrect and should only be used for gaming and entertainment purposes only."*

Denise laughing, "Frank, I get your point, get on with it."

"Okay, Denise, now that you know I'm fabricating these stories and that I'm an egotistical attention getter on exposé who hopes to win the fancy of a charming damsel in distress, let me continue."

"I admire your honesty Frank."

"Thanks Denise. Understand what I'm going to tell you is for you to accept or decline, either way, it does not matter to me. For in my world it isn't important if other people refuse to accept the truth but rather that I accept the truth. For merely by the boat of knowledge, one transcends the sea of evil.

Anyway, where I'm going with all this is before 9/11 and just after the failed World Trade Center attack in 1993. When I was training in Huntsville, Alabama, I worked with a bomb technician who I will address as Mr. X. Mr. X was at the World Trade Center right after the explosion in 1993 and he told me firsthand that the area was closely monitored by the F.B.I. and that the bomb technicians were instructed specifically where to go and what to look for and what not to look for.

In essence they were quarantined and confined to certain areas until the F.B.I. allowed them to look elsewhere. This controlling factor is unheard of among bomb technicians at a bomb scene and it led in turn to some bomb technicians to become suspicious of the whole event. Furthermore, what led to the arrests of these alleged Arab terrorists was pointed out to some bomb technicians on where to gather the critical evidence as if the F.B.I. knew in advance where the critical parts were.

Again, this is quite unusual for bomb technicians who are always in charge of the complete bomb scene, but in this case they were being restricted to certain areas and severely chastised for doing otherwise."

"Sounds like you lived an interesting life Frank."

"Thanks, I like to think I do, Denise."

"Well, with all that training you had, what's your take on 9/11, Frank?"

"Denise, let me put it this way, first thing I want to say is that I don't want you to think I'm blowing my horn. I'm just presenting the facts and my observations and opinions, okay? So take it for what it's worth.

In life, there are individuals that have significant experience on a particular subject matter and therefore have a better eye for seeing faults in a story line based on their hands-on experience, intelligence and common sense.

Denise, I'll give you a few examples for a better understanding of what I mean. For example, polygraph examiners are an excellent choice to study deception. This is because their job requires vast amount of experience in the study of the polygraph technique, body language, story consistency; interviewing and interrogation strategies coupled with the polygraph charts.

Any polygraph examiner worth his/her salt should have a better eye for identifying deception then the common man. I mean we are getting paid to reach a diagnostic evaluation on whether an individual is either truthful or deceptive, correct?"

Denise responding, "That's correct."

"What I mean is Denise, truth and deception are a polygraph examiner's venue. Examiners get paid well for their professional and expert diagnosis of the case facts.

I'll use the licensed pilot as my second example; a licensed pilot should have a better understanding on airplanes limitation and its capabilities better then the common man. The pilot should also be able to determine what an airplane looks like at a distance better then the common man in order to prevent airborne collisions, etc.

A Certified Police Officer and a State Licensed Private Investigator for example, should have acquired by their profession; "a suspicious eye" and a better understanding of the inner workings of criminal activity and the criminal mind more then the common man. Also, these sleuths by using their network of intelligent assets and snitches can get an inside track on what is going on and what happened during a particular event of concern.

Moreover, a well-trained high explosive bomb technician should be better suited for finding and discovering an explosive device better then the common man. The high explosive bomb technician should be able to see, analyze and determine that an explosive device has been detonated. He would be best suited for understanding the complexities and the dangers of said devices. He also would be best suited in the manner of how to place and use these devices within their capacities to the utmost. Also a seasoned bomb technician will quickly analyze and be cognitive of the signatures of an amateur bomber as from an expert bomber. Furthermore, the bomb technician should be able to distinguish a military operation that has gone awry from an amateur operation of prior placed and rigged explosives.

Lastly, a military officer whose military occupation specialty is one trained as an engineer in explosive devices should be familiar with military hardware and explosives used to blow up bridges, roads, airfields and disarm mines to name a few.

In conclusion, any of these individuals trained in any one of these professions that was relevant and applicable to what transpired on September 11, 2001, would have a keener sense of awareness to a self-orchestrated event then the common man.

What I'm stating here Denise is that individuals in these types of professions, per se, have a better eye then the common man. For as the saying goes, "In the land of the blind, the one eyed man is king."

That said, "We the People" are led to believe that two airplanes with passengers hit the World Trade Center building and a passenger plane hit the Pentagon yet where were all the bodies?

You know Denise; I've been involved in rescue operations in major crashes. In particular the airplane crash at Detroit Metropolitan Airport where I worked the body retrieval detail along with numerous other police officials. That detail had to be the ugliest and most grisly scene one would ever want to be involved in. Take my word for it that there were bodies there Denise, to horrific to describe.

Lastly, we are told heroic individuals overwhelmed alleged Arab terrorists in an airplane that ultimately crashed in Pennsylvania.

Would you agree with what I said so far, Denise?"

"Well, Frank, the short story line on 9/11 seems right as I recall the events. However, I totally agree in every example you gave that a well-trained individual with experience and common sense in a particular field that is relevant to the event has a better eye overall then the common man. Yes, I would agree with that."

"Good, Denise, because obviously 9/11 involved a criminal act and was conducted by criminal minds. A conspiracy! This criminal act was a military operation created by military people whose involvement caused significant pain, suffering and death to innocent American people. This criminal act misled the American people into an illegal war where their brave sons and daughters were deceived into murdering innocent people whose only fault was that they were born standing over oil.

My people, the American people, on 9/11, were murdered in cold blood. While, "We the People" watched women with their dresses on fire jump from the towers from between shard glass windows unto their death.

We were told this act-involved airplanes, Arab terrorists and some alleged Saudi Arabian mastermind known as Osama bin Laden.

It is alleged that Osama bin Laden with his questionable military experience in tactics was hiding somewhere in a cave with water dripping down on his head while scorpions and centipedes were running over his feet had somehow concocted this grandiose aerial assault on our nation.

It is further alleged, as we are led to believe, that Osama was writing his master plan with a stick on a cave wall. All the while he was mustering up his fat clueless lieutenants in their white shawls who could barely differentiate between a camel and a lamb yet could somehow mastermind a plan such as 9/11.

It is against this backdrop that, "We the People" are told that Osama and his primitive tribal chiefs who were most probably resting up against a U.S. made World War II Jeep equipped with a 50-caliber machine gun and its encrusted bullet links, could somehow fire cruise missiles against the Pentagon. Moreover, these same clueless leaders were able to use American fighter planes, F-16`s as a matter-of-fact, to shoot down Flight 93 with American made heat seeking missiles while shutting down our air defense systems.

Should I continue, Denise or am I rocking your world too much?"

"Continue, Frank, but you're scaring me? Are you serious or did you just miss your medication?" (Laughing)

"Hell yes, I'm serious, (laughing) no, I didn't skip my meds. At the time of the 9/11 attack it is believed the United States Space Command fired a penetrating missile a bunker buster missile, believed to be a derivative of the GBU-28 into the World Trade Center.

Then shortly thereafter, some fifth columnist businessman with a vested interest in one of the towers uses bomb technician verbiage.

He states, "Pull it" which initiates a firing train that mysteriously drops the World Trade Center Building 7 on itself.

All this is done without the building being touched by an alleged terrorist explosive device and was identical to a controlled demolition.

The phrase "pull it" is a bomb technician's terminology to initiate a firing train for an explosive device or devices to be initiated, activated and detonated.

We are then told that suspected Saudi Arabian individuals flew some so-called hijacked airplanes into the towers. The United States Government begins a war on Iraq and Afghanistan, based in part, on weapons of mass destruction that never existed and despite Pope John Paul II plea that this war was immoral and God was not on President Bush's side.

We then send the flower of our youth against the assumed Arab infidels into an undeclared war by Congress, against Iraq and Afghanistan who had nothing to do with 9/11.

We attack Iraq, who had no weapons of mass destruction. We also attack Afghanistan whose only gift to humanity since the beginning of time was to emerge out of the Stone Age.

We then attack these two nations with all of our American middle and poor class children, while our United States Congress's children with their "safety in privilege" are nowhere to be found on the front lines in this "alleged war on terror." All the while our children are fighting and dying chasing fictitious phantoms known as, Al-Qaeda by mainstream media that is controlled mainly by the Zionist.

During the time of the attack on Iraq, Israel hits Baghdad with three to five micro-nukes in downtown Baghdad that was confirmed by U.S. satellites. All the while American brave fighting men and women are misdirected into murdering 1,000,000 innocent Iraqi's and Afghanistan's peasants, again whose only curse was that they were standing over oil.

But the Crème de la crème is that our kids who were in the beginning innocent have come home after being misdirected into murdering 1,000,000 peasants who were in fact only defending their homeland. These same American soldiers then go to church, genuflect and receive the body and blood of Jesus Christ, as if nothing had ever happened."

"Frank, are you saying the Arabs did not do 9/11?"

"That's correct, Denise, the Arabs did not do 9/11, they couldn't have, they did not have the capability or the capacity. The wars a fraud and this homeland security FSA is another fraud to the bone."

"When did you first suspect this Frank, that the Arabs didn't do 9/11?"

"When 9/11 happened Denise, I was working up in my house's attic. My late wife, Ruth, yelled to me to come down and have dinner with my two daughters. As I was making my way down from the attic a news bulletin suddenly came out over the television and stated a plane had just hit the World Trade Center.

Being a licensed pilot with high performance aircraft training background the first thing that came to my mind was that some pilot had made a terrible mistake. Within minutes of the second plane hitting the World Trade Center, I kissed my wife and daughters for I knew a war with someone was coming and it was going to get ugly. Of course the rant went forth, "Kill the Arabs and let God sort them out," but I knew from experience and intuition that the Arabs were made the patsies.

Though my late wife, Ruth, told me before she died that I was suspicious the war on terror was a fraud on the first day. Yet there were flaws and gaps in the government version and I became totally convinced that the war was a fraud within seven days after 9/11. I knew then based on all my experience and training that this war on terror was an orchestrated event conducted in part by our own intelligent agencies against our own people, the American people, known as *We the People*."

Again, Denise, I refer you back to what I just stated regarding an individual who has specialized training and hands-on-experience in specific areas relative to an unusual event that has occurred. It is reasonable to conclude that this individual may unravel a mystery unseen by the untrained eye even though he may not have been privy to or made totally aware of all of the facts.

That said, lets say an individual has various specialized training in more then one area that is all relevant to a particular event that has just occurred. It would appear on the surface that this individual, due to past training and experience in multiple disciplines, could mentally see the façade of a orchestrated event even though his observation may be based on only a limited number of case facts presented to him.

Moreover, if this individual knows the basics and the particulars of his specialized training, he therefore is capable of "connecting the dots" of this particular event in question much better then the common man. This individual with his multi-faceted training and experience would quickly realize that the correct version of the event would have to add up to $2 + 2 = 4$ yet the government's version of $757 + 93 = 4$ doesn't hold water. It would therefore become readily apparent that elements within our government were deliberately misleading the American people into an orchestrated war in order to murder innocent people and steal their assets.

Understand Denise the government's version of the 9/11 events was not meant for the minority of critical thinkers who can think on their feet or have a keen mind or sharp eye. No, not at all, for it was meant for the masses of the innocent young who feel it is their duty to rally around the flag and the "sheeple" who have been duped, hoodwinked, snookered and bamboozled since birth."

"Couple questions Frank? You mentioned a missile hit the Pentagon instead of a plane, how did you derive at that? You then mentioned plane Flight 93 was shot down by an American plane, how did that happened? Which begs the questions, *who are the terrorist* and why does FSA have to shake us down on our plane flights?"

"I'll try to explain this as clearly as I can and I'll try to avoid all the technical explanations, Denise. To begin with, I have to go back in time to explain some of this.

First lets talk about what is believed to have hit the Pentagon for it was definitely not a plane.

Back around 1971 or so, I was in Marine Corp Pilot Training flying high performance T-28B`s Trojans and the Vietnam armed version A-28`s out of Naval Air Station, Whiting Field, Florida. During pilot training at Pensacola Naval Air Station, we were given aircraft identification classes that the United States Navy felt was very important in the event we encountered hostile aircraft while deployed. During this identification class a lot of the student aviators had problems distinguishing various aircrafts from different angles. As a matter-of-fact a lot of students were in danger of failing the class and there was concern by the training instructors that this large amount of failures would be a reflection on their teaching skills.

However, I didn't find the class difficult at all for I was scoring 96% to 100% on all the examinations without studying and everyone began to wonder how I was doing it. The instructors were watching me closely because they believed I was cheating or had an inside track on the tests. As the class continued I found out that I held the highest score among the fifty or so naval aviators. Finally, the instructors became so concerned when my scores were so above the norm that they decided to address this issue with me in private and called me out of class.

Denise, there were four men in the hallway waiting for me with questions. Two of the men were my military instructors and the other two were unknown civilian personnel who were standing in the background and listening to our conversation.

The first thing they asked was, "Lt. Legion are you cheating in our class?"

I told them, "What? No sir, do you want me to take the exams again? I'll take them right now without studying to prove it?"

They didn't answer my question but then they asked me, "Did you ever belong to any aviation groups prior to joining the Marine Corps?"

I told them, "No."

At this time one of the civilians asked me straight out, "Lt. Legion have you ever been trained by a foreign power?"

Now mad, I answered, "No, of course not."

I was then questioned by the other civilian who asked me directly, "Lt. Legion have you ever been trained by the Russians or employed by them?"

I said, "No, and what's this questioning all about?"

The military instructor came forth and stated, "Lt. Legion we thought you were an enemy agent, a spy, because of your excellent identification of NATO aircraft. However, your identification scores of Soviet and Chinese aircraft under all types of lighting conditions and angles went off the charts."

I then replied, "So? Are you trying to tell me because I have the highest score in my aircraft identification class that I have to be questioned like this?"

The ranking civilian came forward and stated, "Lt. Legion, we apologize for questioning you like this and being suspicious of your high grades. However, we would like to set the record straight and make you aware of the fact that you are not only the highest in your class in aircraft identification but you have obtained the highest grade in aircraft identification in the *history of Naval and Marine Aviation!*"

I was speechless and astonished, wondering if I heard him right so I then asked, "Excuse me sir, did you say I have the highest score ever obtained by all the Naval and Marine aviators in history?"

The civilian stated, "That's correct Lieutenant, the highest ever in Naval Aviation!"

"Wow, I'm speechless, sir. No wonder you questioned me," I said.

The lead civilian then asked me, "Did you do this by study alone?"

"No, sir," I said. "I built about five hundred model planes as a young boy and I would play with them for hours on end with my boyhood friends in simulated dogfights."

They all laughed and the lead civilian now smiling answered, "No wonder, why didn't we think of that? Your free to go Lieutenant."

I looked over at Denise and stated, "What I'm trying to say is that I can identify aircraft better then the common man and perhaps better then many aviators. Though I'm not claiming perfection by any means, but in the field of aircraft identification I like to believe I'm an expert witness.

Fast-forward to September 11, 2001 in which a closed circuit camera film had escaped confiscation by a three-letter agency and was left at the gas station on the Pentagon grounds during 9/11. The film revealed to me that a Boeing 757 aircraft did not strike the Pentagon but an American made and controlled *"RQ-4 Global Hawk" or a hybrid variant of it did."*

"Wow, if your hypothesis or theory is true it's frightening, Frank."

"Hypothesis or theory, Denise? (Laughing) Let me continue.

Regarding Flight 93 and according to my intelligence network, things apparently went wrong with the overall 9/11-conspiracy plan. Flight 93, is believed in certain circles to have been heading to the White House or the Capitol Building on a collision course. The Adjutant General of North Dakota who was outside the loop of power of those who were controlling this conspiracy, scrambled American made F-16's to intercept Flight 93. Believing Flight 93 was taken over by fictitious Arab terrorists, he gave the order to shoot down Flight 93 to the American pilots flying American planes with American missiles."

"Frank, that's terrible, how can this be? Have you ever considered gathering all the facts you know and publish a book?"

"Who would read it, Denise? Just you?"

"Frank, who knows?"

"Well, Denise, the American people would be shocked to know that it appears our own intelligence agency upper echelon are controlled by the Skull and Bones, which is a derivative powers of the Illuminati. Furthermore, the international Zionist bankers, the figurehead Queen mother and her gangster associates including the Saudi Arabians are the designers of all this.

Our air defense was in stand down mode so our three letter intelligence agencies with their cohorts in crime, the Israeli and Saudi Arabian hierarchy, could murder in cold blood 3,000 Americans at the World Trade Center on that sunny day, September 11, 2001.

Moreover, the "five dancing Israeli's" along with sixty-four or more Israeli agents who were on the scene were arrested by U.S. federal agents, *given polygraphs and failed.*

*Yet, President Bush and Vice President Cheney who are both treasonous co-conspirators in this mass murder of their own people further let the Israelis go home and what better place to hide Satan's children but among God's people.*

The name Skull and Bones is a derivative of the Illuminati whose favorite son, President Bush and his draft dodger friend in crime, Vice President Dick Cheney are serial killers on the lam. They should be tried for high treason including their whole cabinet, at that time, by the American people and if convicted hung on the White House lawn.

I only wish Denise that I could be allowed by the American people to *interrogate and polygraph these criminals at large who walk and talk in their three piece suits on national television before "We the People."*

I would pay my own way and go it alone if need be for the only thing that I would ask, "We the People" is that they keep the cameras rolling throughout the whole interrogation process.

I can bring down these fat cats, Denise, and I would prove to the American people that what I just said is true.

Yet, I know this can never happen because these "perfectly possessed people" are protected by privilege.

Nevertheless, I'm absolutely certain that if they examined President Bush, Vice President Cheney, their whole cabinet with their cohorts in crime the Saudi's and Israelis, all would fail.

I'm absolutely certain they would all fail; all of them, and hopefully a spontaneous combustion throughout America would reach a critical mass and lead to a revolution by the working middle class to rid themselves of these demonic entities who walk in human form.

*For if justice cannot be served, then let the heavens fall*, Denise."

"I'm speechless Frank, any more stories before we reach the prison? I almost forgot why we were going to Ohio?"

"Well, Denise, yes there is and it starts this way, I sent a letter to the head of a three-letter agency based on the continual observation of a few community leaders that I observed while working undercover in Dearborn, Michigan's, southend.

This area was the largest Arab concentration in North America and as a patriot; I felt it was my duty to inform this seat of power about this growing menace that was misleading the Arab people. The letter, I sent, was in regards to a concern I perceived as a communist infestation among a few groups of Arab organizations that were developing at the grass root level. These groups in question I believed were attempting to sway the Arab community in the wrong direction and would cause great harm to the image of the Arab people as a whole.

Unbeknown to me, my letter sent to the three-letter agency created concern among them and they forwarded that letter up the chain of command. Ultimately, it arrived at a meeting of the *Joint Chiefs of Staff and when it was presented to them, I'm quoting now a federal agent, "it turned their heads."*

Without further adieu, a C.I.A. agent paid me a visit. As we talked, he informed me that according to an article that appeared in a well-known business newspaper that is distributed throughout the country and specifically on Wall Street, that this newspaper ran an article on the front page describing how the C.I.A. failed in the 1970's to organize spy rings within the Arab American community. These spy rings would become a linked network back to the foreign shores of Arab governments, which in turn would assist the United States Government against hostile enemies both domestic and abroad. The agent further stated due to my extensive work and life proximity in this area would I be available to help them? I stated I would consider it to be my patriotic duty by helping my country against all of its enemies both foreign and domestic.

He stated, "good" then departed and would be in touch.

After a period of time while working, "undercover" in the industrial area near the Ford Rouge Plant, I was called by the agent and was offered a dinner date the following day.

When I met the agent he bought me dinner and we began to talk. He stated he wanted to know if he could recruit my services by helping to build a spy network for espionage purposes for the United States of America. He stated this loud enough at the dinner table that it could have been heard by anyone within the dining area. This I found to be unusual and wondered why he would want all the businessmen at the surrounding dinner tables to overhear his conversation if they so desired.

In bomb terminology I felt he hit a trip wire and flags started to go up in my head for my military background has taught me that, "loose lips sink ships" yet this guy could care less who heard him. He then asked if I could draft up a list of particular individuals within the Arab community who could work covertly for the C.I.A. and be a means for the United States government to funnel information back and forth from the Middle East to Langley, Virginia.

Before I answered him, I asked for his identification and he showed me a bona fide Central Intelligence Agency badge with photo identification. I then showed him my identification and while he was looking at my badge I scanned the dinner tables around me and I noticed that numerous individuals had the look of a military or police demeanor.

Perhaps Denise it was just a coincidence, but flags again started going up in my mind and I became more concerned. Then as the agent handed me back my badge he then stated he would take me off my police status and inform all my bosses that I would be working for the Central Intelligence Agency until their objective was met.

I then told him, I would help my country though I did not want my bosses to know whom I was working for or with. He stated that they could not put me on the payroll but considered what I was doing an act of patriotic duty and that they would work on the quiet with me.

Though at this time I was torn between my patriotism and my police suspicions of this guy, I reluctantly agreed. Still I wondered when I looked at this agent for he was just too pretty, too spiffy, an Ivy League pretty boy with tasseled shoes. In other words, he was an educated momma's boy who never got his hands dirty in his life. Besides bringing him Arab American patriots from the rank and file of the community I told him that there were international drug dealers that I had arrested that during "street" interrogations they had informed me that they were part of a drug network already in place which was running from Dearborn, Michigan to Lebanon and beyond.

As a matter-of-fact, Denise, the drug dealers considered me to run polygraphs on their drug running mules and would pay me well.

Anyway, I asked the C.I.A. agent if I brought him these drug dealers that were my snitches or my eyes and ears within the community would they be punished? His response, "No" surprised me and I was left with the impression that he preferred them and their dealing in drugs apparently was not a C.I.A. concern.

Can you believe that, Denise? Hell, even now I still can't believe that, but it's true. As I looked at him I could not help but think since when does the C.I.A. not care about drugs coming into this country? Or is the rumor true from the black community that drug dealing in the inner cities supports "black op projects" and leads back to the doorstep of the C.I.A. I mean I couldn't help but think if I was being played a patsy to maintain the global elites status quo or further their agenda of colonialism.

I then thanked him for the dinner and he thanked me for my cooperation. As I walked away from the restaurant I rubbernecked back and looked to see if any of the businessmen I observed around my table was talking to the agent man, but I saw nothing. Crossing the parking lot I couldn't help but feel uneasy for it was an intuitive feeling I had, a cop's sixth sense, that this guy was too pretty.

A lifetime of working the streets alone in various disciplines with the genetic variance of human animals has taught me that this guy was different. I didn't like him, for intuitively I didn't trust him or find him sincere and when I walked away from him I felt I needed to take a shower. It was like I went to bed with some smelly crack headed

59

slut that the eighteen-wheeler truckers pick up. For I felt my love of country and it's people was perhaps *again* being used in the most vile of ways, which was to be exploited and discarded as an expendable asset.

After a period of time the C.I.A. agent called me and I informed him via secured telephone and letter that I had contacted Arab-American individuals who were patriotic in and willing to assist. I further informed him that I was also in contact with certain drug dealers who were already involved in established drugs routes from Dearborn, Michigan to the Middle East.

Finally, at the coordinated times and places I handed the C.I.A. agent over to Arab American patriots, ex-military preferred, whom I trusted who were very visible activists in the community. They all stated they were interested in helping me after I explained the details in depth to them and that they would help build the spy network from Dearborn, Michigan to the Middle East. So the spy network was in place and activated according to those activists I had contacted later. Yet as a proper courtesy and to put my contacts on notice I informed them of my distrust for this agent man and for the greater part they all agreed with me. A short time later the activists informed me that they were doing work for the agent man and they would take it from there. They then stated that since I was officially out of the loop they would appreciate it if I didn't question them further regarding the operation in which I agreed.

Shortly thereafter, the world observes on the television and reads on the front page of all major newspapers how alleged Arab terrorists brought down the "Clipper Maid of the Seas" over Lockerbie, Scotland.

Allegedly some Libyan terrorist in another orchestrated and phony lone gunman scenario, had allegedly planted high explosives in a radio that was aboard the plane "Clipper Maid of the Seas" which belonged to some poor Arab kid who died in the crash.

The father of the kid of course vehemently denied the allegations of his son's involvement in the terrorist act and ultimately the kid was exonerated.

The United States responds with air strikes against Libya nearly killing Muammar al-Gaddafi, who was "holed up" in a tent in the desert though they did kill his son.

You see Denise, Arabs are assumed to be terrorists and further perceived as Anti-American, but this is not true, for they are very patriotic about America."

"Okay, Frank, your point?"

My point, Denise, is do you remember where that boy was from who the U.S. intelligence agencies accused of being involved in the terrorist act of killing all the passengers on "Clipper Maid of the Seas" but he could not testify to their accusations because he died in the crash?"

"No, Frank, I don't recall?"

*"Denise, he was from Dearborn, Michigan."*

"Really, wow…hmmm. But, Frank, it could just be a coincidence."

"Perhaps, but on matters of this importance I don't believe in coincidence Denise.

There is not a day that goes by that I don't say to myself how I love my country and its people. Yet I can't help but wonder that doing my patriotic duty did I initiate an idea that wicked men in power manipulated to initiate an unjust war against the Arab people in order to seize their assets? Was all this done so "The Powers That Be" could maintain their seat in power and feed this military industrial complex that President Dwight D. Eisenhower had forewarned us about?

Were the contacts that I made in good faith to help my country establish an espionage ring from Dearborn, Michigan to the Middle East, worth it? In the end, when this operation went into full effect in conjunction with other parallel operations and ultimately played out, was I one of the duped stooges?

I can't help but feel that I was, and that our intelligent agencies are not agencies for the United States of America, *or it's people*, but rather an intelligent collection agency for the global elite in whatever country they reside in. Moreover, was this innocent Arab boy from Dearborn, who had been falsely accused for assisting or allowing explosives to be placed aboard this "Clipper Maid of the Seas" aircraft in truth a victim who had been victimized?

Further, were the patriotic Arab-American activists whom I introduced to the C.I.A. agent to, like myself, just an expendable asset, fall guys and a duped stooges?

I cannot help but feel a sense of betrayal from this Ivy League agent who I think hoodwinked, duped, bamboozled and snookered me."

"Denise, if I'm getting too carried away here just tell me to take a powder and I'll stop to light up my cigar and puff away, okay?"

"Your fine Frank. I prefer you saying what's on your mind then lighting up that rag you call a cigar." (Laughing)

"Dang, Denise, you're the second person who told me that today. Whatever happened to the expression, "Real men smoke?"

"You mean, "Dead men smoked," Frank."

"So that's how it goes, hmm. I guess I got it wrong? Denise, forgive me, but I'm not blowing smoke, no pun intended, but this is what I believe happened to the, "Clipper Maid of the Seas."

"I know you believe in what you're telling me, Frank, and I believe your story is more closer to the truth then what the government's story is."

"Thank you Denise. Let me put it this way, 2+2= 4, right?"

"Right", Denise now looking at me inquisitively.

"The government's story, Denise, pertaining to 9/11 as told to the American people, is equivalent to the formula $757 + 93 = 4$ while my testimony and formula as close as I can get it, is $3 + 2 = 4$. That said, the recipients who hear both of these stories know that both stories being told to them are not totally correct.

But if you are a truth seeker and given only limited information and your searching for the truth, which story are you going to believe?"

"Obviously, based on your example Frank, the story that is closer to $2+2 = 4$, and in this case, it would be yours."

"Thank you again, Denise, and without further adieu let me continue. When this alleged war on terror began, that is after 9/11 on the World Trade Center, the word went out across the nation that the FSA, the Federal Safety Administration would be forming in order to protect airline passengers from alleged Arab terrorists who were everywhere and hiding behind and under everything.

The American people were told or led to believe some man named Osama Bin Laden, again the lone man assassin, masterminded this dreadful attack on American soil and in response to this, the federal government initiated a huge hiring program and Americans were called to the challenge to help thwart this alleged "war on terror" by joining the FSA to help prevent the spread of terrorism and keep the skies safe for Americans.

Against this backdrop, I was informed that among the priorities for the FSA was the hiring of "bomb technicians" with prior training and experience who would be at the top of their list. Of course this makes sense and what better way to look for explosive devices but with the eyes and mind of a bomb technician who does this work on a daily basis.

So I called the Federal Aviation Administration and they informed me that it would seem right that bomb technicians are in high demand. So I applied with the FSA and despite the problems they had of hiring felons, creeping crud, and their low pay, I considered it my patriotic duty *again* to defend my country and it's people once more.

So a short time later I received a letter from the FSA who stated that they were delighted I would consider joining their organization. To the chase, after filling out the paperwork and jumping all the hurdles, I was given a time and date to take a multi-test examination at a Federal location in Detroit, Michigan. When I arrived at the scene I was met by armed federal men who shook me down for weapons then escorted me to the testing center. At the center there were approximately five hundred to a thousand applicants, who from their appearance looked desperate for a job. Our pictures were taken along with fingerprints and we were escorted to our testing tables to begin the testing phase ritual. We were all given folders yet; I noticed mine was an orange color, while everyone around me of those that I could see, had a yellow folder. I assumed it was because I was a bomb technician trained both military and civilian, so I let it go.

The testing phase was in five sections and I was very confident that I would pass the examination because a couple weeks prior I had just completed the United States Custom examination and passed with flying colors awaiting employment. At that time my late wife, Ruth, wanted me to put the bomb squad mentality behind me and become a Customs Agent for a change of pace. Anyway, at the beginning of the testing phase the exam administrator called out if anybody was from the C.I.A.? Obviously, I thought it was some lame joke but I did notice that three of the testing regulators looked only at me.

As a polygraph examiner this was a subtle indicator to me, yet, I was unclear what it meant or was it just a coincidence. Nevertheless this flag that went up in my head compelled me to analyze what this could mean. I then went into a heads up mode to see if I was over reading the indicator or if there was something coming down the road that I had yet to determine.

At this time we were told to start taking the examination on the computer screen that was in front of us. I found it almost laughable as I went through some of the sections; it appeared as if an elementary child could pass the exam. But I rationalized it this way, how else could the government justify affirmative action and social engineering in order to hire the "boom box people" who were so dumb they couldn't tie their shoes or lift up their pants.

So I continued moving through the testing phase at a reasonable pace, constantly thinking the exam had to get harder and harder, but it didn't. So when I got to the math section I was expecting to put my math background of algebra, geometry, trigonometry and calculus into play, yet the test only contained simple multiplication. I thought to myself, is this examination for real or did I inadvertently enter into a testing section of humans with recessive genes?

I mean, Denise, to fail this examination one would have to be an imbecile or dumber then a bag of rocks. A damn pigeon could pass it, except for the last part of bomb identification. When I got to that part, I looked around and I realized that I was way ahead of everybody and I felt good. I knew I could beat everyone hands down and the job would be mine. For the bomb section contained some real subtle pictures of explosive devices that I knew no one would know except a bomb technician.

I chuckled and said to myself, "I'm in" and, "I'm unstoppable" and I'm going to score the highest score in FSA history indeed!

Then as I'm halfway through the bomb section phase *my computer for no apparent reason suddenly shuts off!*

*It shuts off on its own!*

What the hell just happened, I said to myself? What's going on here? Moments later the computer comes back on and before me is a blank screen. I'm dumbfounded, I looked around and everyone else's computer was working fine. I look over at this black sister next to me whose typing away with her two-inch gold engraved fingernails. She has a look on her face like she's not sure if she's at the salon or cashing bad checks at some inner city bar…but her computer is working fine.

Now I'm upset and concerned and wondered who hit the reset button on my computer, but there was no one around. In desperation and becoming ill at ease I called out for a testing administrator. When the black sister arrives, I tell her the problem. She tells me, she will have the main administrator look into it and perhaps reset my computer.

After ten minutes of waiting, my computer resets itself and kicks back on and all my input data is gone! The black female returns and states my computer has been reset though I tell her my input data is gone. She then states, "Well they said your computer is reset," then walks away.

Denise, I am now sitting in a stupor saying to myself, am I dumber then a bag of rocks? Or am I brain dead so bad that resuscitation is not required. I felt like I was a hominid with recessive genes and dumber then a pigeon.

What the hell just happened? Who the hell is in charge here? Mass confusion sets in and I somehow become lost in time and space. I stand up and hand in my examination to the main testing administrator who says to me, *you failed!*

I'm crushed and ready to live out the rest of my life in heartbreak hotel, I mean I'm done like dinner, a loser, a raggedy man. I asked him where did I fail? He states one of the sections though he didn't know which one. I felt like hell, I can't explain this and how the hell am I going to explain this to my wife, Ruth.

She's a lot like you, Denise; she doesn't want any alibi or story but only, "Did you get the job, honey?" plain and simple. As I stood there looking at the administrator he calls over two federal agents and they are told to escort me to the elevator to get me off the premise. As they were escorting me, I felt like I was a "Dead man walking" on death row. As I'm standing there with a federal agent on each side of me, I still wondered what happened? Was it coincidence? Was it a power outage? Or did I in my arrogance just plain fail? I didn't know.

As I looked down at my shoes awaiting the elevator, I looked back to the testing area and seen a young twenty-five year old white girl shaking the hand of the administrator. I heard him say that she was given the job of supervisor for bomb detection.

With a blank mind I stood there for a moment when suddenly the elevator doors open and myself along with two black men enter into the elevator. The federal agents tell the black men and myself that we are to go down to the first floor and then please exit the building immediately.

I'm saying to myself, damn, I came to take an examination to prevent the American people from being placed in harms way but I'm being treated like I committed a homicide.

As I entered the elevator, the two black men looked at me, as if they were angels, as I continued looking down at the floor pretending I didn't see their intense stare. The doors closed on the elevator and as I continued looking at the floor and the lighted elevator buttons; one of the black men stated to me as if he knew.

"They got you too, man?"

I said, "Beg, your pardon?"

He repeated, "They got you too man?"

Fuming, I stated, "I'm a bomb technician, how can this be that I failed?"

He stated, "I'm an arsonist investigator and my associate here is a retired police supervisor and we both failed."

I stated, "How can this be? I mean bomb technicians are absolutely necessary for bomb detection to keep Americans safe. Further, arson investigators are needed for incendiary devices, fire catalysts and explosive devices. Police officers are needed for their suspicious eye in dealing with criminals on a daily basis, yet they gave the job to some young inexperienced white girl, how can this be?

The black man stated, "They didn't want us man, they didn't want us."

It was then my blood boiled, Denise, I realized that I had been played. The blood rushed to my head, and I knew, "The government doesn't want to know, they don't want eyes to see their dirty work or their misdeeds. They want dummies! How deep is the rabbit hole and how refined are they? For they knew we were coming and they knew they had to fail us. It was then Denise, at that moment in time and for the very few times in my life, I was scared, matter-of-fact, I was terrified for I knew our country was under siege."

"Frank, in light of all the stories you just told me, when you take them as a whole, it is frightening what your saying. I mean your implying the government is much more sophisticated, deviant and deeper in their operations then what, "We the People," are led to believe they are.  If I further understand you right, you're claiming the government is not just monitoring and controlling groups but controlling individuals on a micro scale. Am I right?"

"Yes, Denise that's what I'm saying."

"So, Frank what you perceive has happened to you based on your training, experience, common sense and knowledge is that the government is social engineering the whole human populace.  To what ends, Frank?"

"You're a sweetheart, Denise, if you can see all that?  What the government is creating is a cast system, a ruling class and a slave class, where the ruling class governs through invisibility.

In this way they can avoid from being detected and maintain their seat in power, *forever*!  Like I said earlier, Denise, they don't want critical thinkers, they want human vegetables that tote the company line at all cost while they lavish their life in luxury. They use our daughters for procreation and for their meat and our sons to cull them through war by stepping on a land mine for the home team.

I believe this theory, I really do!  So I apologize to you for not being able to explain it to you in less then a million words or less."

"I hear you, Frank, reality is not what we perceive it to be.  Further, we humans are ruled apparently by some higher and hidden order."

"Yes, Denise that's what I see in part and it's closer to the truth then what the government is telling us.  For they, the power, are the government, which is why we are always enslaved.

Anyway, now that I told you practically my life story and not playing tit for tat, what made you become a polygraph examiner, Denise?"

"Oh, my story is simple Frank; my prior husbands were chronic liars.  I hate liars."

"Well, Denise, I believe the shortest distance between two points is not a straight line but the truth of the matter.

Anyway, we are getting close to the prison so we better refocus on our case today."

"Back to this case Frank, I'm all for going for the jugular on this matter to see if Rosemary cracks."

"It's your case, Denise, I'll be your wingman. The first question we should ask Rosemary is:

Did you participate or encourage your boyfriend "Trooper" in the wiring of, or placement of the pipe bomb in your husband's vehicle?

This would show if she was involved in a conspiracy, if she helped plan with someone to kill her husband and perhaps the remote possibility that she did design the improvised explosive device herself."

"Okay on the first question, Frank, then I would like to ask her this for question two:

On the evening prior to the explosion were you aware that "Trooper" was placing an explosive device in your husband's vehicle?"

"Good, for this in part would double cover the first question Denise and again shed light on if she planned or had help from someone. Then ask her question three:

Prior to the explosion were you ever aware that "Trooper" placed a pipe bomb in your husband's vehicle?

This would reveal guilty knowledge, conspiracy, plus her direct involvement."

"Then I think the next best question to ask her, Frank, is question four:

Did you plan, conspire or help "Trooper" in any way, to kill your husband?

Also question five:

Did you lie during testimony that your reason for bringing your husband's vehicle to "Troopers" house was only to examine a muffler?"

I replied, "Excellent, Denise, for the first question is a catchall question regarding any involvement whatsoever.

The second question would reveal any omissions, denials and lies regarding her testimony with respect to her story line. The last question we ask Denise is identical to the third question. In this way, hopefully, we can pass her or fail her conclusively on this question.

<u>Prior to the explosion were you ever aware that "Trooper" placed a pipe bomb in your husband's vehicle?</u>

Truthfully speaking, I don't think she made the bomb. If Rosemary did make the bomb, she had to be cognizant of its devastating potential. Otherwise, she's one very lucky or very stupid woman who apparently did not know or did not care to know of the imminent dangers involved.

However, she may have been forewarned that there was a timer on the pipe bomb, which would arm a pressure sensitive switch. What I'm saying Denise is that, Rosemary, may have known she had just so much time to get her vehicle to her location before the improvised explosive device automatically armed itself.

Or she could have had a remote and when she got home she pressed the button remotely from a distance, which armed the explosive device making it ready to fire.

Lastly, she could have had a manual-arming switch and when she got home she clicked the switch, which armed and activated the explosive device so that the next person to sit in the car would blow up.

Yet, maybe she's an airhead and drove the vehicle unaware what she was sitting on. There are many theories, but in the end we have to go by what the polygraph questions reveal and her situational awareness.

This interview is crucial and both of us tag teaming her should find flaws in her defense and gaps in her story. My feelings again about this matter are that this has to be a conspiracy and the real killer or *other* killers are still out there.

If Rosemary is in for life and her attorney is taking a long shot on a retrial, which is her only chance to go free, it would seem to me that Rosemary would confess to us to what really happened?

Yet we cannot exclude the possibility that she has been telling us the truth all along or the possibility that she was the target of the pipe bomb. Who knows? Anyway, our best weapon, again, will be in our interrogation to see if there are any gaps or inconsistencies in her testimony. Finally, on a critical case like this where a life is at stake the polygraph charts will be of an extreme importance for our diagnostic evaluation, therefore, we must not make any errors.

Even though, Denise, we may have pity on her situation we must keep an emotionless poker face throughout the examination.

You play the concerned compassionate cop and I'll play the hard cop with attitude."

"That shouldn't be hard for you Frank." (Laughing)

"You know, my late wife, Ruth, always said that to me." (Laughing)

Arriving at Oregon Ohio Federal Prison, Denise and I went through the usual hurdles by getting just short of a strip search and our equipment inventoried. The administrator was insistent that I sign my full name on the ledger, as Frank Tam Legion, so I could be held responsible for anything that went awry. We were then taken within the walls and it appeared all the prisoners were in some type of lock down each to their own cell. As I walked down the corridor I could not help but notice the sad and lonely eyes of the female prisoners. What a waste of womanhood.

As we approached our location the guard opened Rosemary's cell and we walked into cramped quarters where we introduced ourselves. The whole cell was an open structure surrounded by plexiglas instead of bars, definitely minimizing privacy.

When I looked at Rosemary, I observed a well-developed white female with long beautiful auburn hair and a good face structure. She looked about 35 years old, 5`9 and about 120 pounds. Rosemary was a beauty, soft spoken with a thousand-yard stare that made her look bewildered and depressed with a life sentence hanging over her. What a waste I said to myself of this beautiful woman. It's a pity she will never know a man again. She was caged now and standing in quicksand while grabbing at anything she could. She knew this was her last chance, all or nothing, and hoped the polygraph examination in conjunction with other evidence would grant her a retrial.

As we started the questioning, I sat in the back of the cell watching Rosemary's body language, which wasn't hard to do. Scanning for subtle countermeasures and visual signs of deception, I awaited the opening move.

Denise took the lead and I watched these two beauties square off as if they were playing Russian roulette.

"Rosemary, again, I'm Denise and this is my associate, Frank. We are here on behalf of your attorney, "Buck" Travis, to determine via a polygraph examination your involvement, if any, into the murder of your husband, Mumdu. We are going to waive your legal rights because legal counsel already represents you. If you have a problem at any time within the polygraph examination let us know. That said, at anytime in this investigation if you feel you don't want to continue with the examination, we will stop and leave. Are we good to go so far?"

"Yes, Denise I'm ready and understand."

"Good, because Rosemary we are going to ask you a bunch of questions and the polygraph examination will take about two to three hours. At anytime, if you have to go to the bathroom, we will call for the guard and leave until your're ready to call us back. That said, let's start the examination even though your attorney has supplied most of the answers, we still have a few questions that need to be answered."

Rosemary looking at the floor stated "Okay."

As Denise pulled out the attorney's transcript, "It is my understanding you are facing a life sentence for the alleged murder of your husband, Mumdu. Further, you have been in this female facility for eight years. Is this correct?"

Despondent, Rosemary answered. "Yes."

Denise looking at a health form, "What is your medical condition?"

"I am a diabetic, Denise, and I'm on stomach medication for nervousness."

"Alright Rosemary, have you ever taken a polygraph examination before or have you read on the ways and means to attempt to defeat the polygraph technique? Be advised, any attempt that is interpreted as a countermeasure on your part is an automatic failure."

"No, Denise, I have not taken a polygraph examination before and I don't plan on countering the exam."

"Rosemary, have you ever been treated by a psychiatrist?"

"Yes, numerous times. In my youth, I was a rebellious teenager and troublemaker. But it was never anything major and I was never diagnosed with anything."

"Rosemary, have you ever been arrested?"

"Yes, this case for Murder One and Robbery Armed years ago, but I was placed on probation."

"Have you done drugs?"

"Yes, cocaine a couple dozen times and marijuana."

"What do you think of yourself, Rosemary?"

"I'm a pretty good person and I like to think I have a good heart."

"Have you ever been falsely accused of something you did not do?"

"Just this charge, Denise."

"Rosemary, you have been found guilty in a trial by jury for the wiring and the placement of a pipe bomb under your husband's vehicle. Ultimately, this pipe bomb not only killed your husband but cut him in two. Do you still deny this?"

Rosemary's face was becoming flush, "Yes, I still deny this. I did not murder my husband nor did I wire and place a pipe bomb under his car seat."

Denise staring at Rosemary's twitching hands, "Did you and "Trooper" have a romantic relationship?"

Rosemary hesitating but fearful of lying, "Yes."

"Did Mumdu and you have money problems?"

Rosemary, looking at a passing guard who inquisitively looked within her cell, "Yes."

"Rosemary, were you worried when you drove your vehicle from Lansing, Michigan to Toledo, Ohio that the pipe bomb would explode and maim you for life."

Rosemary stating spontaneously, "I didn't know it was there at that time."

I then jumped in as Denise looked down at the attorney's transcript, "Were you concerned when you made that pipe bomb that it could explode on you."

"No sir, I didn't make it."

"What kind of gunpowder or fuse did you use?"

"I said I didn't make it, sir. Otherwise, I'm sorry…I don't understand."

"C'mon Rosemary, your playing dumb and wasting our time."

"I'm not wasting your time, sir. I wouldn't have hired an attorney and spent $20,000 dollars of my parent's money just to lie to you now. Again, I didn't see a bomb or help place a bomb in my vehicle and then drive it home."

"Well, Rosemary, how did the pipe bomb get there?"

"I don't know, I really don't."

Denise returned to take the lead, "When you took the car over to "Troopers" garage did he not work under the hood and interior of the car?"

"I don't know what he was doing. I was just there for five minutes. I brought it there for muffler repair work."

"Now listen carefully Rosemary, did he tell you what he was doing?"

"No, and I didn't ask."

I jumped in before Denise could respond, "Bullshit! You knew what "Trooper" was doing. C'mon, that's why your doing life. Lifting the hood up and going into the cars interior to do muffler work, you got to be shitting me. He was wiring the explosive device to the solenoid switch, wasn't he?"

"Solenoid switch, what's that, sir? I didn't do it."

Denise came back, "Then who did?"

"I don't know."

I jumped back in, "Bullshit, what do you mean you don't know, Rosemary? What do you think pipe bombs are, factory issued with every vehicle? It was either you or "Trooper" who did it, or both. Hello, do the math…or was there another player in the game? Did anyone work on your vehicle besides your squeeze, "Trooper?""

"No sir, "Trooper" is not my squeeze. No one worked on my vehicle except "Trooper.""

Denise asked inquisitively, "Okay, then either you murdered your husband or "Trooper" did. Otherwise you two conspired together to murder him, right?"

"I didn't murder my husband."

I then asked Rosemary, "Did you help to murder your husband?"

"Of course not."

I responded, "Of course not? What are you shitting me? Lady, then why are you doing life in prison? Apparently the judge and jury thought it was obvious."

Denise shot back, "Did you plan to murder your husband?"

"No."

"Do you know who murdered your husband?"

"No! How many times do I have to tell you, people? Damn it, I didn't murder my husband."

I then told Rosemary, "Our job is real simple lady, exonerate the innocent and fail the deceptive.

Your husband, Mumdu, has been cut in two sweetheart and someone murdered him. Rosemary, someone placed a pipe bomb, known as an Improvised Explosive Device in your vehicle to kill someone. Your vehicle, okay! You were the last one to drive the vehicle from your lover's house! You arrived home and parked the vehicle in your driveway after a ninety-mile trek with a highly unstable explosive device underneath your ass without any concern? The car sat there until the following morning when your husband entered the vehicle. At that time your husband engaged the starter that activated the solenoid and completed the circuit. This in turn detonated the explosive device beneath the vehicles drivers seat and killed your husband instantly. And you're telling me your clueless?

Lady, I may have been born during the day, but not yesterday. Hey look, you can stay here for life and I don't care. For at the end of the day I'm going home to have a beer, how about you Rosemary?"

Rosemary started to cry, "I didn't kill my husband! I didn't kill him, I loved Mumdu and I loved "Trooper" in a different way. Give me the polygraph examination right now."

Denise looking at Rosemary's hands shaking, "How do you think the examination will come out?"

"That I'm telling the truth!"

"Did you participate or encourage your boyfriend "Trooper" in the wiring of, or placement of the pipe bomb in your husband's vehicle?"

"No!"

"On the evening prior to the explosion were you aware that "Trooper" was placing an explosive device in your husband's vehicle?"

"No!"

"Prior to the explosion were you ever aware that "Trooper" placed a pipe bomb in your husband's vehicle?"

"No!"

"Did you plan, conspire or help "Trooper" in anyway, to kill your husband?"

"No!"

"Did you lie during testimony that your reason for bringing your husbands vehicle to "Troopers" house was only to examine a muffler?"

"No!"

"Again: Prior to the explosion were you ever aware that "Trooper" placed a pipe bomb in your husband's vehicle?"

"No!"

"Have you told us the truth to the best of your knowledge and belief?"

"Yes!"

"Are you ready for testing?"

"Yes!"

After about two hours and a battery of tests, the examination was concluded. Denise looked at me with a surprised look, one of which that I have seen many times in my career. As I looked over the charts with Denise, it became self-evident and unanimous in our diagnostic evaluation that a conclusion could be determined.

As Denise looked at Rosemary, she put her hand on Rosemary's shoulder and softly stated, "Rosemary, rather then leave you in suspense to worry and make your stomach situation worse then what it already is, Frank and I have reached the same conclusion. Our finding Rosemary is that we believe you told the truth to the best of your knowledge and belief, passing your examination to all the relevant questions we asked you. Congratulations!"

Rosemary started crying, "Thank you...thank you very much."

Denise replied, "Your welcome."

As I smiled at Rosemary, "Good luck to you, Rosemary; I hope this along with other evidence presented to the Ohio State Supreme Court will lead to a retrial for you."

Denise responded, "We will notify your attorney today and send him a report tomorrow."

Rosemary while still crying got up and placed her head on my shoulder and said, "Thank you for coming."

I said, "Your welcome sweetheart and goodbye."

I then yelled out, "Guard!"

As we left the facility and headed back to Luna Pier, we were both convinced that an innocent person had been wrongfully imprisoned and we would notify her attorney that we would testify to that fact and further request an immediate retrial.

As we headed north up I-75 to Michigan, I asked Denise, "What do you think about heading over to Canal Street to The Cove Inn for dinner and a drink. I'll buy, while we write this report."

"That's sounds good to me, Frank."

When we got back to Luna Pier, we headed down Main Street to the inlet canal that opened into Lake Erie. The Cove Inn was usually a nice quaint bar overlooking an inlet canal that meandered out into Lake Erie. However this time, we were fortunate enough to find a couple of empty seats in an already crowded place. The locals were mellow due to happy hour starting about three hours before our arrival and were singing, "Missing You," by the Rolling Stones. The whole place was rocking as we laughed and waved at familiar faces that were three sheets to the wind.

We both decided to order a perch dinner with shrimp cocktail as an appetizer. As I began drinking my cold beer, Denise got a glass of red wine as we discussed the case.

"Well, Frank, what do you think of us finding her innocent when she was found guilty by a trial by jury?

Were the case results what you expected or were you blindsided?"

"Not blindsided, Denise. The facts and allegations just didn't add up for Rosemary to do something like this. Rosemary apparently was kept out of the loop for whatever reason and that killer or killers are still on the loose.

Hopefully, if she is granted a retrial the judge and jury will review the facts presented more carefully and consider our bomb technician's testimony coupled with the polygraph results."

"I think the jury made a mistake, Frank, by believing somehow she was an accomplice in the bomb making directly. We now know she had nothing to do with the construction of the pipe bomb. Furthermore, as we speculated before, whose to say she wasn't the target of the pipe bomb."

"Denise, this is what I know and I'm not trying to blow my own horn either. Two trained bomb technicians thinking independently at different times intuitively and instantaneously reach the same conclusion that Rosemary did not make the bomb. This opinion is based on our specific hands-on training, experience, knowledge and common sense.

You see this case should have been before a judge *only,* with numerous bomb technicians taking the stand as expert witnesses. The judge and the bomb technicians would have solved this case alone and reached a more proper conclusion then what the jury did. But as things go, when that A.T.F. bomb technician was sworn unto the sanctity of the stand, he had to be recognized as an expert witness. That means he has special knowledge or training that ordinary people do not possess. Apparently, the judge and jury did not understand the A.T.F. bomb technician's testimony on pipe bombs or its implications.

Rosemary, by her spur-of-the-moment utterance stated she did not make the bomb and also spontaneously stated that she had been falsely accused of this charge. She was clueless on the bomb makeup from our questioning which was confirmed in her court testimony. Further, if she did make the bomb why would she drive ninety miles to her home with this unstable I.E.D. beneath her seat? That's crazy. Also, unless she was diagnosed mentally insane which she had not been, why again would she ride ninety miles to her home with the explosive device directly under her seat?"

"I agree, Frank, that no sane woman who wanted to kill her husband would do such a thing."

"Absolutely, Denise, if you wanted to kill either one of your ex-husbands with a bomb would you drive a vehicle with a device like that under your seat? Hell no, you wouldn't. But the bomb was there and the bomb did go off in Mumdu's driveway.

Further, the bomb killed her husband, Mumdu. Mumdu was killed the next day, after Rosemary drove their vehicle ninety miles. Someone put it there! Someone armed it and activated it! Someone had the expertise of solenoids, batteries, ignitions, wirings and explosives!

Now if it wasn't put in place up in Lansing then it had to be put in place during the night after Rosemary parked the vehicle. Which means what? That the bomber during the dead of night placed the explosive I.E.D. under the vehicle while Mumdu and Rosemary were sleeping. The bomber had to place this I.E.D. in Mumdu`s driveway in the dark of night without a flashlight. How could the bomber place this unstable explosive device under the seat and without making any sound while connecting it to the solenoid? Further, the bomber did this without lifting the car hood or opening the car door and without disturbing Mumdu or his neighbors.

If you can believe that, I got a bridge to sell you on the moon made of cheese. Bullshit period! Total Bullshit!"

"I absolutely agree, Frank. To me the answer is simple; Rosemary did not understand pressure switches, gunpowder, arming switches, remotes and solenoids during our two-hour investigation. She couldn't have done it and she's innocent, for even the charts show she had no guilty knowledge or involvement in a conspiracy. She's innocent as far as we polygraph examiners are concerned. I like to think or believe that we arrived at a more accurate conclusion then the judge and jury did. Moreover, I would love to go into greater detail regarding the possibility of a third player, or more being involved. I mean who has the most to gain from the death of Rosemary's husband? Rosemary is doing life in prison, which doesn't sound like a gain to me for anyone. Rosemary loses, Mumdu loses, "Trooper" loses and the children lose. Who won, that sure is a mystery to me?"

"Yes, Denise, who won, that is the question? Moreover, there had to be a controlling mechanism, a timer, a remote device or an arming switch on that pipe bomb …had to be.

My theory is that Rosemary did not place the pipe bomb in the car, but her boyfriend did or an associate did. In this way it would explain why she was so clueless about the explosive makeup of a pipe bomb.

But seeing that she drove her car home it stands to reason that there was some type of timer, that is, an arming device that would activate after a prescribed period of time. Yet, even with a timer how many women do you think would sit over a pipe bomb for ninety miles especially if they knew it was in place and armed to explode?

None, I suspect.

Again, Rosemary didn't have a clue because her boyfriend, "Trooper" or his accomplice did not tell her what they were doing. Most probably she was told they would take care of her problem and "Mumdu in their own way." Rosemary probably didn't know what was meant by that and probably thought it was going to be "a hit" or shooting on her husband.

Therefore, she probably felt it would be wise to stay away from her vehicle from the moment she parked it in the evening until the following morning.

Look at the question, the critical question, we asked in the exam: <u>Prior to the explosion were you ever aware that "Trooper" placed a pipe bomb in your husband's vehicle?</u>

She answered, "No!" She answered no five times and she passed it every time, plus she passed all the other questions. She is innocent of making the bomb and she is innocent of knowing that the bomb was there in her vehicle. She is innocent of knowing who made the bomb and what they were making. This is why she rode the vehicle home and placed herself in such a precarious situation. The bomb had a timer on it. She didn't murder her husband, her boyfriend did or his associate did! She is innocent and passed her entire exam, yet she is doing time for life!"

"Oh, I agree she is innocent, Frank, but what's that say about the legal system who sentenced her for life?"

"Well, Denise, the jury system makes mistakes at times and they're only as good as the evidence that is presented to them and/or their capacity to understand that evidence presented.

Apparently, the judge and jury did not give enough credit to the expert A.T.F. explosive bomb technician's testimony and nor did they understand the evidence presented.

In this case the judge and jury, I believe, made a terrible mistake here. I hope the Ohio Supreme Court grants her application for leave to appeal, or remands this case to a trial court for a new trial."

"I hope so, Frank."

"Another glass of wine, Denise?"

"If you have another beer."

"That'll work."

## *Chapter 4- Whose on First?*

While at Luna Pier the following day, Denise was finishing up and processing the bomber report when she began discussing the outcome of our diagnostic evaluation with Rosemary's attorney. From the tone of Denise's conversation it appeared Rosemary's attorney was happily surprised and thankful.

As I was watching Denise and trying to locate my Robusto cigars, Coco called me about our two youngest investigators in the field, Tracy and Kelly.

Tracy and Kelly were on temporary assignment from our Maumee Bay, Ohio investigative office. They were Ed`s, grandnieces, and for the moment they were dispatched to cases in western Indiana, a few miles southwest of Indianapolis.

These sisters were as beautiful as ever, actually stunning and should have been models instead of investigators. Tracy, "The Princess" as she was known was 28 years old, well groomed, slender and a beautiful brunette with an olive complexion.

While Kelly, known, as "Calico Kitty" was a 25-year-old, well developed, long legged blonde with hazel eyes and downright gorgeous.

Both girls had sweet personalities, especially Kelly, but both at times were like two cats on catnip, actually crazy. The girls were head turners and when they walked out on Luna Pier they would strut their stuff as if they were on some Paris "catwalk."

I was amused observing the expressions of the young men as these two beauties walked by them. My-my, I would chuckle; there wasn't a young man whose head wouldn't turn or heart pitter-patter when these two sweeties walk by them.

Both girls were educated and registered nurses but for some damn reason, during the spur of the moment, they decided to try their luck as investigators which they perceived as an adventurous lifestyle and much preferred over the life style of helping people within a sanitized hospital.

Ed told me to watch them and watch them closely because both girls were mischievous as hell. They would get lazy and sloppy at times during an examination or sometimes do a half ass job by leaving their clients somewhere between elsewhere and nowhere.

Matter-of-fact, if they were not watched they could just walk off on a Friday afternoon in the middle of an investigation like a "wildcat strike" in the factory. I mean, they were gone in a New York second and felt like it was no big deal to return when they felt like it. They were total party animals and believed work could wait. They were always fighting with their boyfriends and brought their relationship problems into the office, which was a no-no.

Ed and I warned them to keep their personal relationship problems with their boyfriends out of the office. Even though they referred to Ed as "Gramps" and me as uncle they still wouldn't listen to us. If I had it my way they both would have been sent to our Bolles Harbor office or Flat Rock office, which was designated for promising young investigators. But since they were relatives of Ed, he felt obligated and sent them to our Maumee Bay Office to gather experience from the seasoned investigators.

Funny though, "Big Don", who was the boss down there was rumored to be on sedatives from these two "dollies." So after a private discussion with Ed, he had them transferred up here to Luna Pier to help with our caseload and to monitor their progress.

The girls had become overloaded and assigned six to seven cases from a large law firm in Indiana whose attorneys did not want local examiners to test their clients due to privacy and sensitivity concerns. The girls were instructed to handle the first case first, then work their way numerically down the line as each case was handed to them, instead they took all the cases at once and everything was out of "good order."

It gets like that in this business sometimes, "when it rains it pours".

According to Coco, all the cases were sex issues, the first case was a Roman Catholic Priest who got mixed up with a female parishioner who was suing the Church and pressing for criminal charges against the ordained priest.

The second case was a high profile front-page news politician that allegedly liked playing, "**tit** for tat" with the lady secretaries.

The third case was an airline pilot from a major carrier who was sweating out sexual allegations from an airline stewardess who he claims is black mailing him.

The fourth case was from a strange suspicious man, *profession unknown*, who thought his lady friend, or whoever, was running around on him. Details were scant at best, which usually implies that the case is much deeper then what we were being informed about.

The fifth case was a young man, music major, who had criminal sexual charges pending against him by a young girls mother. I would ask myself why would the young mans attorney stress his client was a music major and what did it matter? I know the devil is in the details but sexual perverts come in all shapes and sizes.

Then the sixth case was a computer analyst who had eight counts of criminal sexual charges for committing cunninglingus and felatio with three five-year-old girls. Even though this case reeks to high heaven it's going to be difficult to hold my neutrality if it's true.

Lastly, the seventh case was on a man every one called "the grub" who allegedly molested his girlfriend's daughter and the results would determine if they get married.

The fate of these examinees has been placed into the hands of the polygraph examiners who now carry the burden of, *"The Switchman"*, who no doubt will change the fate of individuals one way or the other.

For as Jesus said on the cross, "Father into thy hands I commend my spirit."

As polygraph examiners, and not by choice, we are cast into these predicaments where we are forced to alter the examinee's destiny. It's a huge responsibility, for we examiners have to play the role of King Solomon in the Temple to determine, *who lives, who dies!*

This profession has no room for inexperienced, unscrupulous or cold-hearted examiners who lack empathy for people when their lives are at stake.

For altering the destiny of just one man or woman could in truth have a cascading affect on humanity and it's destiny.

Therefore, I am well aware that the King of Heaven who knows all things and looks down upon this predicament is cognizant of the fact that one of His children has been brought before me to be judged.

Moreover, that this child of God's, whose life, liberty and pursuit of happiness has been placed into my hands is a position that no reasonable or prudent man would take lightly.

Therefore, I must judge fairly at all times and to the utmost of my abilities…or quit the profession!

*It is imperative I get to the truth of the matter at all cost…least I stand in judgment!*

Looking down at the floor and returning to reality, I said to myself, I've been played while Ed slipped out the back door on vacation to leave me holding this bag of responsibility.

But as I looked out the window towards Luna Pier, I could see the smoke from the stacks of the Great Lake freighters heading to Pennsylvania and Minnesota to pick up coal and iron ore. There are times in my life when I wish I were a sailor or mere deck hand on one of those ships instead of playing the role of judge and jury.

As I depart from my daydream and return to reality I realize that the polygrapher's caseload is like the weather that's always changing. We polygraph examiners evolve by being immersed in constantly changing predicaments that covers the whole spectrum of the human drama. This in turn expands our perspective on life and develops wisdom in which I presume is the reason why we are here.

Now where's my Robusto cigar and matches?

When Coco yells out, "Frank you have calls on line one and two."

As I push the phone button for line one, I state in proper phone etiquette, "Luna Pier Polygraph Services and Private Investigations Incorporated. Frank Legion speaking, how can I help you?"

As soon as I heard her voice, I recognized it was the secretary, Delores, from the Maumee Bay, Ohio, Investigative Branch calling.

"Frank, Big Don wants to know if you can handle an alleged criminal sexual conduct case regarding a surgeon and a nurse. She's claiming he molested her and he's claiming she's extorting him. A high profile he-she situation."

Responding, "Why can't you people handle it, Delores, we're drowning in cases here."

Delores shot back, "Our examiner Eddie was assigned the case but the surgeon in question is a friend of his, Frank. This case is going to be front-page news Frank and Big

Don wants experience on this high profile case. The surgeon's attorney wants to cut this false allegation off at the pass before it hits the airwaves."

"Delores, hold on. Tell Big Don that Denise should be clear of her bomber case soon, okay. Further, Ed pulled Darryl from the Toledo Harbor Light office to help in our caseload. But he still isn't clear of his present case of international ships that are bringing in contaminated birds with the avian influenza virus to Michigan's Chinese restaurants that are trying to save a buck.

At this time I don't know if I can spare one seasoned investigator let alone two, Delores."

"Frank," Delores in a raised voice, "Big Don is going to be pissed if two seasoned investigators don't handle this case."

I reinstated my position, "Delores, all my investigators are in the field on cases.

I myself have around six cases that I am involved in for the next couple of days. Tell Big Don that's the best Luna Pier can do."

In a huff, Delores responded, " I don't think that's good enough."

I shot back, "It may not be good enough Delores but that's the best I can do."

Pushing line two, "Luna Pier Polygraph Services and Private Investigations Incorporated, Frank Legion speaking."

A black mans voice responded, "Mister, I need a polygraph examination."

I responded, "Okay, at the moment I'm going out on a case sir so leave the details and your phone number with our secretary, okay. I'll transfer you back."

The black man replied, "Mister, my wife's dead!"

I stated, "Say again sir?"

"My wife is dead," said the black man, "I woke up in bed and she has a knife in her throat and she is dead. I didn't kill her. She's dead, mister."

Bewildered, I asked, "Where is she now?"

He replied, "She's in my bed now with a knife in her throat and I didn't do it. I need to take a polygraph test to show I didn't kill her."

Thinking this guy could be a victim of a home invasion, drug raid gone wrong or a murder rap in the first-degree, I inquired where he was.

I asked. "What city you calling from?"

He replied, "Detroit."

"Now listen" I responded, "The first thing you have to do is call 911 and get a squad car out there to investigate your situation. Further ask for an ambulance, can you do that right now? What phone are you calling from?"

He replied, "A payphone."

"Call 911 right now, ask for an ambulance. You hear me?"

"Click"

"Hello, hello, the guy hung up on me, imagine that." as I looked at Coco, "He probably murdered his wife. Coco, we got caller ID on that phone call?"

"No Frank." as Coco checked her phone, "You want me to call Detroit and notify them?"

"Coco, tell Detroit that one of our investigators just picked up a call pertaining to an alleged murder of a possible black female and run the audiotapes by them on our conversation, then let them take over from there, okay?"

"Okay Frank, I'll call Detroit Beaubien and give it to them, it's their venue."

"That'll work Coco", as the phone rang, "Luna Pier Polygraph Services and Private Investigations Incorporated, Frank Legion speaking."

"Hi, Uncle Frank this is Tracy. Kelly and I want to know when are we leaving for Terre Haute, Indiana?"

"Hi, Tracy, were leaving this afternoon after lunch. I'll see you both at 1:00 pm sharp. Why don't you girls get a room together at the Best Eastern Inn and get me one on the same floor.

I want to remind you and Kelly that there is a convention down there, so no late partying to the wee hours of the morning. I'm not going to baby-sit you two girls through six or seven exams, okay."

"Uncle Frank, why would you say something like that, you always think we're goofing off?"

"Tracy, I'm just saying this okay. So we have an understanding now. If you or Kelly shows up buzzed or mellow just before examination time, I'm going to rat you out to big Don and Ed. I'm serious!"

"Sheesh, Uncle Frank, you used to be fun, now your just an old crab."

"Well, Tracy, I know you two like to party.  I want to make sure we're all reading from the same sheet of music so there will be no misunderstanding when I send one or both of you home crying on the Greyhound bus.

Tracy, I may have been born during the day but not yesterday, okay?"

"Weren't you ever young, Uncle Frank?"

"No, Tracy, I was born old and I'll see you at 1 p.m."

"Boy uncle, it looks like a fun time, gosh."

At one o'clock, Tracy, Kelly and myself headed to Indiana, a couple hours drive from Luna Pier to the "Indiana Young Defenders Firm," in Terre Haute.

While heading outbound we discussed the various cases where I informed them of certain pitfalls and dangers to be ever mindful of, for it was for their benefit not mine.

I also discussed with them what on earth were they thinking when they took all six to seven cases from the attorney firm over the phone without first discussing the matter with a senior investigator or Coco.

Listening to their reason was like walking in a big circle during a rainstorm, you end up back where you started and still out in the cold.

Anyway, after further adieu it was apparent that we had one big mess on our hands.  Furthermore, I did not want to get into a discussion with them because I knew intuitively the results would be irrational, heated and nonproductive.

I informed Kelly and Tracy, as I do all young investigators to be aware that as a State Licensed Private Investigator, a P.I., or a State Licensed Polygraph Examiner that one has to be aware that there are grave risks in this profession.  An investigator must be ever vigilant when they are conducting a polygraph examination in an examinee's home.

That is, think safety first, because when things go wrong and they do at times, the examinee has the jump on you.  Even though you laid down the rules regarding the polygraph examination, your still playing in their place of abode and they know the layout of the land and where the guns are.

I further advised them not to assume their clients are always stable for some are dangerously unstable and can even be sociopath or psychopaths.  I reviewed key points in their training and schooling and what to look out for by studying the examinee's body language, mental condition and psychological condition as best you can prior to running the examination.

If you feel extremely uncomfortable with the examinees mannerism in anyway then come up with any excuse you can to get out of their place of abode and to safety. Depending on the case you administer, always ask if they do drugs or have a felony criminal record.

Moreover, ask if they have they been treated or diagnosed by a psychiatrist and if there are there any guns in the house. Red flags should go up if any of these four questions are answered in the affirmative which means you should consider departing the premises.

If all these factors exist simultaneously, and they do at times, then like a pilot in a burning jet, pull that Martin-Baker ejection seat handle and your out of there. Moreover, if all questions are answered yes, it is company policy that you leave without question in order to prevent yourself from being placed in harms way.

Further, always tell someone at Luna Pier where you are going and when you are entering a residence threshold. When the exam is finished notify Luna Pier that you have completed the examination when you are outside the residence and that you are now returning to the office.

Lastly, thirty plus years of running polygraph examinations in people's homes *of which I believe I am the only examiner in the country that has done this that is verifiable* has taught me to pack a gun if you feel uncomfortable about an upcoming examination.

Be aware that when you the polygraph examiner show up at the client's door, he may be predisposed to kill you. You must realize that if the client is cognizant of the fact that he may be exposed for his misdeeds by a polygraph examination then *they may murder you.*

Remember that you may be alone with one or more people who may be unfriendly and secretly have a gun on you which has happened to me many times in the past. You must be strong then, hold your ground like a rabid pit bull for it is better to be judged by twelve then carried by six.

Be advised, *for my guns are not virgin to notches* that you may have to draw your gun or shoot your way out and kill or be killed in the process. This is the life of the polygraph examiner and private investigator who at times pay with their life from being crippled by an angry husband who runs you over with his vehicle after failing his infidelity exam to being mortared in Iraq for interrogating enemy combatants. Like phantoms, ghosts and shadows we are there but rarely seen.

This is what the polygraph examiner is faced with which my late wife; Ruth, was terrified every time I had to enter a private home instead of an attorney's office.

For it just isn't the black neighborhoods that concerned me, but rather any household that contained a gun or a butcher knife.

Be advised that the marital cases were the most dangerous of all polygraph examinations in a residence home.

For the deceptive examinee is aware that they might lose their house, their spouse, their children, their money and their way of life. For them to silence you or attempt to pay you off is not an unreasonable option to them. Remember, those clients who are about to lose everything are least likely to mourn your passing.

*This is how I feed my family. Yes, this is how I fed my family for thirty plus years, so that they would not be impoverished or in want and that justice could be served to help the broken, forsaken, downtrodden and imprisoned souls of humanity whose life didn't matter since the day they were born and who are screaming out for justice.*

As I looked over at the faces of the girls they had a somber look about themselves as if they were now uncertain if this lifestyle was for them, or whether to return back to their profession of nursing.

As we were approaching the scene, I informed the girls that I'd be handling the Roman Catholic priest and the politician. Tracy had the airline pilot and maybe the suspicious husband. Kelly had the young man who was charged with rape and a person known as only "the grub".

Then depending on how things went, for it was always uncertain, I would most probably take the computer analyst case, a known pedophile.

Though the exact "batting order and time frames" of the polygraph examination locations were always subject to change we all accepted it as part of the polygraph profession.

I further advised the girls that we would be there for a couple days either way so to make the best of it.

Lastly, I informed the girls I'd be with them from time to time to monitor their progress and check for any problem areas that may arise.

I had to constantly watch these sweeties because they have been known to stampede out of the office in a New York second with a shop till you drop *ittis*.

When we finally got to the firm, I talked to the Attorney in charge, Mr. Cabman, about the polygraph examinations that we could run today at his office or their designated location. Then the rest of the examinations that were still outstanding would be administered over the next couple of days at their office or client's location.

## *Chapter 5 - The Priest before Pilot*

As we started our examinations at the attorney's office, Tracy took the room with the airline pilot, Kelly took the room with a young man known only as the, "music major" while I took the conference room with the Roman Catholic priest.

Needless to say we had our hands full and I would walk into each examiners test site and introduce ourselves and discuss the examinee's particular problem at hand. I made no qualms about this, that is, all questions must be answered truthfully and any deviation from that constitutes a failure. I told the girls to waive all the legal paperwork for we examiners are here at the behest of their attorneys.

At this time we commenced our examinations.

I started in with the good priest John, whom I secretly called the "Good Pope John the 23$^{rd}$" after what the Vatican referred to him as. The good pope had failed to honor a mandate, better known as the third secret of Fatima, from heaven by the Virgin Mary. He was instructed to reveal the secret in 1960 to the people of the earth and abide by it in order to avoid suffering and chastisement upon human kind. He was further instructed to consecrate Russia to the Virgin Mary's sacred heart, which would bring peace to the world.

He refused to honor the mandate of heaven, as all subsequent popes did thereafter with their dubious alibis, thereby damming humanity to a period of chastisement in which we are currently under.

As I began my examination, I asked the good Father John what he was crying about and would he briefly explain his case to me and if needed we would later go over the gory details if any.

So, Father John began by saying between the sobs how his dedication to God, his livelihood and his parish are in jeopardy due to allegations that he molested and manhandled a woman. According to the allegation, the woman in question claimed the priest groped her breasts and buttocks and gave her herpes some 30 years ago. This in turn allegedly led to her demise that caused her to go through five failed marriages...........I laughed.

I asked, "You mean to tell me father, this lady in question had five failed marriages all due to the allegation that you grabbed her breasts and buttocks and gave her herpes some thirty years ago? Was this an ongoing event or a one time deal, Father?"

Father John replied crying, "Mr. Legion, I don't even remember this incident. I don't even know if I knew her then. As far as I know she is making this whole story up and suing me for money."

I stated, "You know father there are a lot of problems with the Roman Catholic Church right now and a lot of priests have violated their oath of office. I'm not saying your one of them father, but I want you to know that if your being set up by some dame that's trying to extort you and/or the Catholic Church for money...I'm not going to sacrifice you or the church to this extortionist.

But remember you have to tell me the truth, the whole truth in order to pass your examination. Because if your one of these priests who have knowingly violated your sacred position which you swore to uphold before God...I'm going to fail you without mercy. Do we have an understanding?" as I handed him my handkerchief.

"Yes sir." responded the priest.

As I looked at him, I wondered if I just walked into another pervert that has cost Catholic parishioners, a half of billion dollars, from America alone to defend pedophiles in out of court settlements or a godly man falsely accused. Either way he was going to sink or swim on his own accord. I for one was not going to uphold an institution such as the Vatican, which has failed terribly to clean their own house from these "wolves in sheep clothing. No, let them burn in hell in this life as a preparation for an eternity in hell.

But then again, I may have a God fearing man here who is being persecuted by the powers of darkness. I cannot imagine anything worse then to wrongfully fail a human angel of God's then hand him over to the dark side. That thought alone terrified me, for always in the polygraph profession prudence and caution must prevail. If a polygraph examiner must error during an examination, he must error on the side of justice.

It's a shame though, that if this priest turns out to be innocent, it again shows me how a lifelong noble career can be extinguished in the blink of an eye by the whims and fancy of some misguided individual. These extortionists, wolves in sheep's clothing, could care less if they are robbing stewards of Christ who upon this rock Jesus must call his church.

Looking at the floor and digressing for a second I pondered why would GOD of heaven even want to send his only son, Jesus Christ, to save such a hopeless race as mankind. It appears to me sometimes that mankind is not lost but has chosen evil and we are the original fallen angels of old who were thrown out of heaven like lightning with the demons, Satan and Lucifer and cast down to earth.

"Father John, you and I understand that the Roman Catholic Church has begun a zero tolerance policy for sexually abusive priests. The prior U.S. Conference of Catholic Bishops meeting in Dallas has attempted to respond to Catholics across the country that are demanding swift and harsh penalties for sexually abusive priests who have harmed children even once.

That said five current priests in your area have been banished from their ministries, according to our intelligence report. Moreover, including you, thirteen additional priests are under consideration for banishment according to the County Prosecutor Michael Digit.

Now, Father John, I'm not in the business of ruining a man's career just because he grabbed a little titty and ass to relieve the pressures of his "fire down below." You see Father John, if you fail with me as a private polygraph examiner, your attorney can defend you better by not allowing you to take an examination with the public examiner for the prosecutor. For if you fail your examination with the public examiner followed by his subsequent investigation a warrant may be issued for your arrest and you may ultimately end up in trial. Father John, have you ever seen the dumb look on most jurors and are you aware of the public sentiment towards priests nowadays with this "one strike rule." What I'm saying is do you really want to place yourself in harms way?

So if you square with me now and confess that somewhere back then your innermost id got the best of you and you did what you had to do to relieve your pressures on your mind, you'll feel better about yourself.

Personally speaking, I really don't give a rat's ass on what you did thirty years ago because I myself may have grabbed a women's breast back then for fun, I mean it's irresistible and boys will be boys."

The priest looked at me with sorrowful eyes and stated, "Mr. Legion as I said before, I don't remember the incident and I didn't do it."

"Okay, Father John is that your final answer before I commence the polygraph examination?"

"Yes, it is Mr. Legion and I am aware that my livelihood due to these false allegations that has assassinated my character has been placed in your hands and my attorneys."

As I glanced down at the floor again, I pondered again upon what Father John just said and reflected back to the words of Jesus Christ, "Father unto your hands I commend my spirit."

"All right Father John, the prosecutors complaint here shows the lady in question was somewhere between 13 to 18 years old at the time of the groping. You know if she's underage at the time and there is no statue of limitations, you're in a world of hurt. You know that right?"

"I didn't do it Mr. Legion."

"So then Father John, you categorically deny the allegation that you grabbed her breasts and buttocks or gave her herpes because you did not have sex with her?

Moreover, you are requesting to take the polygraph examination on your own volition and free will in order to clear yourself from these trumped up charges. Is that correct?"

"Yes, Mr. Legion, I feel this polygraph examination is the only option I have to exonerate myself and to show that the lady in question is targeting me for extortion purposes just because I am an ordained priest within the Roman Catholic Church.

It is like its open season on the priesthood, yet it is not that I am guilty but that I am presumed guilty because of my position now and must prove my innocence."

"Well, Father John, as far as I am concerned the polygraph examination is comparable to the law of the land of which I must start you in a neutral position prior to taking the examination. For there must be a presumption of innocence that examinees have right from the get go, which is, your innocent until proven guilty. So don't assume just because you are a priest, that I presume your guilty prior to your examination. No, sir… you stand before me now as innocent, that is, not guilty unless I can prove you otherwise.

*Father like you, your mission in life is to save souls by converting souls to Christianity and Baptizing them in the name of the Father, Son and Holy Ghost.*

*My mission in life is to free the captive innocent from the snarls and traps of Satanic forces that walk the earth with men who attempt to share their bodies and darken their tormented souls.*

*For in the kingdom of heaven, as agents of Jesus Christ, we all have our place and mission as directed by this King of Kings. To free the souls of the captive innocent, so that they may live and know justice, until the return of this rightful King who will sit upon the throne in Jerusalem. To this end is my prime directive."*

"That's refreshing to hear, Mr. Legion, apparently you're a God fearing man?"

" I am…. that I am, Father John, though some people studying your case would think in light of all the terrible crimes being perpetrated in society nowadays, that your case is just a slap on the wrist.

Yet, I know as Jesus Christ stood before Pilot, you now stand before me *in judgment,* which is an undertaking that I take very seriously. Despite the screams of the ignorant crowds who are led by their blind guides they still call for your head.

For as you can see, Father John, you have been dragged before me already condemned, mocked and psychologically scourged. Your accusers have come for your very soul as they scream out with outstretched and tormented hands, *"Give us Barabbas"* and to you they say, *"Crucify him, for we have no god but Caesar!"*

For I know and you know that, *"The servant cannot be greater then the maste*r." For if they crucified HIM, can you expect anything better then to be falsely accused and spiritually and psychologically put to death?"

"Mr. Legion, I'm terrified of what the outcome could be."

"Indeed you should be, though I am a total stranger to you yet I have a direct bearing on your life's work *by freeing you or having you crucified.*

But as we've been told Jesus Christ judges fairly…. then so must I. I hope that brings some comfort to you, now that you understand my position and perspective."

"Yes it does, Mr. Legion."

"Nevertheless, Father John, today, you are going on a journey, like a gladiator fighting in the ring in the coliseum of life. For at the end of the day you stand before this legal system that is the figurative form of Emperor Nero with a verdict of thumbs up or thumbs down. So to you who stand before me in this mockery of justice that may ultimately destroy your soul, I salute you!

For today only *"The truth shall set you free."*

Do you know, *"What is truth?"* Father John?"

"Yes... I'm ready Mr. Legion, I did nothing wrong."

"Then, Father John, I'm going to start by asking you a battery of questions about your health and lifestyle. To begin with, the paperwork required that gives me authority to examine you has been waived by your attorney, so I'll begin by asking you this.

What is your education?"

"I have a masters degree in Divinity."

"Have you ever been treated by a psychiatrist?"

"No, I have not."

"Do you have any health issues I should be aware of?"

"I have had open heart surgery 6 years ago."

"How long have you been a priest?"

"Mr. Legion, I have been a priest for 41 years at St. Luke's parish."

"Have you ever been arrested?"

"No, I have not."

"Have you ever taken any non-prescribed drugs?"

"No, I have not."

"What is the worst thing that has happened to you in your life?"

"This incident has been a traumatic affair Mr. Legion."

"Have you ever been falsely accused, Father John?"

He answered spontaneously, "Yes, this incident I'm definitely falsely accused."

"I now want to ask you Father John, test questions your attorney and I have agreed upon that is relevant to your case."

"Alright."

"During the time you were at St. Luke's parish did you ever intentionally touch the lady in question's buttocks?"

"No."

"During the time you were at St. Luke's parish did you ever intentionally fondle the lady in question's breasts?"

"No."

"During the time you were at St. Luke's parish did you ever talk to the lady in question in a sexual manner?"

"No."

"Did you ever touch the lady in question in anyway for sexual gratification?"

"No."

"Are the allegations of the lady in question sexual abuse true?"

"No."

"Not connected with this case have you ever been engaged in any unusual sexual activity?"

"I'm sorry can you repeat that Mr. Legion"

"Not connected with this case have you ever been engaged in any unusual sexual activity?"

"Ahhhh...I am not sure I...."

"You're not a pervert, are you Father John?"

"Ahhh...of course not."

"Then your answer is no."

"Ahhh...hmm..okay."

"Not connected with this case have you ever told an important lie to someone who trusted you?"

"Important lie?  Wow...that's a tough one Mr. Legion.... important lie?"

"Father John, your not a liar for gods sake, you're a man of the cloth and your taking a polygraph examination.  Are you lying to me today?  If you are, you failed your exam already."

"I mean..."

"You don't tell important lies, do you Father John?"

"No, I do not."

"Then your answer would be no."

"Hmm…okay."

"Have you told me the absolute and complete truth about everything?"

"Yes…. those last two questions though were a bit confusing, Mr. Legion."

"Are you ready for testing, Father John."

"Yes, I am."

As I went through the battery of tests, the polygrams revealed that Father John had told the truth to the best of his knowledge and belief to all the relevant questions.

Moreover, the entire questions fell into the positive quadrant that was due to the proper application of the polygraph technique that is based on research, which claims an accuracy percentile of 85% to 95%.

Father John stated the only questions that bothered him were the questions about "important lies", for he wasn't certain what an important lie was and the question about "unusual sexual activity", he thought was weird.

I just laughed and informed him that those questions were incorporated into the polygraph technique as a safeguard to protect the innocent.

Needless to say, Father John was relieved as I patted him on the shoulder and informed him that he did excellent. I informed Father John's, attorney that they have a green light from me to go before a public polygraph examiner and that the priest should do very well.

In my thirty years of running polygraph examinations only twice did a public examiner come up with a different result then I had.

One examiner was from the same Sheriff's department as the examinee who was also a sheriff that I failed for beating his civilian subjects with a flashlight.

The other examiner was from a State Police post that failed a high-ranking police Chief official that I had just passed, who was "clean as a whistle" and who was falsely accused by his ex-girlfriend for domestic violence just because he wouldn't marry her.

I felt this case was in retaliation for a State Police examiner, a lieutenant, who was a byproduct of affirmative action that was arrested for being a drug dealer at the time he had unjustly failed a doctor client of mine. When I reviewed the lieutenant's charts and numerical score it was obvious and self-evident that the lieutenant had unjustly failed an innocent man for the charts corroborated my argument.

At that time I could only imagine how many examinations were thrown in favor of the Lieutenants "homies" and co-conspirators in crime that the thought of it made me sick at heart.

As Father John left the room grateful, I informed him that his honesty and his faith had saved him. He shook my hand and thanked me upon his departure.

As I gathered up the charts and legal papers I decided to see how Tracy was doing with her airline pilot and Kelly with the music major.

## *Chapter 6 - Clutch Cargo*

As I walked down the hallway, I looked into one of the attorney's conference rooms and could see Kelly still in the pretest interview stages explaining the legalities and science of the polygraph technique to this young adult music major with a tuning fork in his hand.

I said to myself, why would he do that? Yet some people are just plain odd as in this case, which brought to mind these words, "Rome burned as Nero played the fiddle."

Suddenly, Tracy stepped out from her conference room as the airline pilot answered a cell phone call from his wife. As Tracy approached me I questioned her as to why she didn't have all phones in the conference room shut off to avoid any outside distraction?

Tracy stated the pilot was waiting for an emergency call from his employer, American Bald Eagle Airlines, regarding allegations from an airline stewardess that claimed he grab her seven year old daughters breast and buttocks aboard the plane just after passengers departed the 727 aircraft.

I asked Tracy what she thought and she stated, "I don't know what to make of it Frank, during the initial pretest interview he sounded sincere. Moreover, his body language and story line looked and sounded real good."

"You think he's had been set up, Tracy?"

" I am not sure, Frank."

"Well, Tracy, let me tell you this before we enter the conference room and start to examine this professional airline pilot.

Obviously we both have had cases where men molest women and many of our cases assisted in getting these male predators off the streets and thrown behind bars, which is what we get paid to do.

However, as in my last case, of which I just completed with this Catholic priest, a great majority of these cases are nothing more then extortion cases, that is, monetary blackmail, nothing more.

In most cases the perpetrator, the female, will not be polygraphed because she is the alleged victim and the burden of proof is left to the man to prove his innocence. That is, he is already guilty and fighting from a premise of guilt and not the presumption of innocence.

Due to liberal changes in most state laws throughout the country almost any domestic violence case the male is assumed to be at fault and is therefore arrested. For the most part, the male is stripped of his integrity; his profession is destroyed and he is disgraced before even having a fair and just hearing or trial. He does not enter the courtroom Tracy, presumed innocent. But rather, he is looked upon as a savage predator or a wife beater who is standing before a judge and jury for crimes he most definitely committed. The gallows, for this man figuratively speaking is already constructed and the noose is already placed around his neck even before his trial is heard.

So, despite all this Satanic and liberal feminist ideals, which in truth has destroyed the family structure and claims every woman is a Cinderella, it just ain't so.

Therefore, one has to know the difference between a female streetwalker screaming rape because of a failure to pay for a "BJ" and an innocent lady being gang raped by inner city savages when her car breaks down on the Detroit expressway.

As with male savages and brutal men, the same percentages of women are as vicious and vile as the men are. These women better known as gold diggers have no good intention in their heart and soul and their prime directive is to find justification for their lifetime of bad moves and failures.

These females are as godless as their male counterpart, for they are destroyers of families and dreams and make children parentless. Furthermore, these vile strumpets could give a rat's ass on sending an innocent man to prison. Because they, Tracy, like the male predator are Satan's own.

During my tenure as a police supervisor where myself and other officers had to enter into the homes of perhaps a thousand or more domestic violence cases, we knew both genders were equally guilty.

But in the beginning we would just separate the combatants and send them out of the house to cool off, which they eventually did. In the scheme of things, the combatants were aware, that the police gave them a chance to cool down and avoid arrest.

So they, the combatants, were aware that we gave them a break and they wouldn't abuse their good fortune until they cooled down and reflected on their problems and that was the end of 99% of these cases.

The marriage was saved for the moment, the combatants became lovers again, and the kids had parents, life was good.

Then one day, regrettably, in a domestic violence case in upstate Michigan, a case of which I was not a part of, the combatants were separated and sent on their separate ways with the understanding to cool down before seeing one another again. Both combatants agreed and went their separate ways, and then the police departed the scene, as all appeared quiet and peaceful.

Unfortunately, this one man hunted down his wife after the police had left and murdered her.

The liberals and the feminists lashed out screaming on how could the police allow this to happen to this poor defenseless woman. So the legislature was forced to change the law to the detriment of any male present at any domestic violence scene.

Now, every time police enter domestic violence domiciles, the male is arrested in almost every case because police discretion has been taken away. Police officers including myself do not want to get sued or be held responsible for some immature male rock band freak or his academia naïve female lover who are most probably drunk and too immature to handle the rigors of their relationship.

So in the end, Tracy, the children suffer and become wards of the state and a tax to the law abiding working man and woman.

To the quick Tracy, the *Wisdom of Solomon* must be applied here and this pilot's life, is literally, in your hands."

"I hear you Uncle Frank. Even though I believe women are much more then a man's chattel, I am not going into this exam predisposed that this airline pilot is a breast and buttocks grabbing pervert, okay?"

"That's all I ask, Tracy, is that this man is looked upon as innocent until proven guilty and not guilty until proven innocent."

"We make a hell of a team, Uncle Frank."

(Laughing) "Ya, right."

As we entered the room, we could see that the pilot had a troubled look on his face, definitely not a good sign before a polygraph examination.

Tracy introduced me, "Mr. John Rocco, this is Mr. Frank Legion, he'll be my assistant in your case today and he will be present throughout this examination."

"Mr. Legion, it is a pleasure to meet you."

"The pleasure is mine, Mr. Rocco."

Tracy then continued with the pretest interview and began with the story line.

"Mr. Rocco, now that I found you suitable for testing and healthy enough to undergo the rigors of a polygraph examination, why don't you tell us in your own words what happened.

But before you do we want to make sure you are aware that polygraph examiners have *attorney client privilege* like doctors, priests, attorneys and private eyes. So everything you say now will be held in strict confidence.

Therefore tell us the whole story and the complete truth to the best of your knowledge and belief."

"I'd be glad to Tracy, but first I want to say I can always get another job somewhere for I am an engineer by trade. However this case is an attack on my moral character and a direct assault on my integrity. For I work with kids and a case like this could destroy the very fabric of my being."

I stated, "Are you worried John, that if the word gets out that people will look upon you as a child molester and pedophile."

"Yes, you hit it on the head, Frank, for in my heart I worry about that," John angrily stated.

"We understand how you feel John and hopefully we can clear it up today," Tracy responded.

"Well nothing against you people but I lost a day of work, I have attorney fees and your examiner fees. All of this came about because a desperate woman is falsely accusing me. I am sick at heart," John explained.

Tracy came back, "We know John that if this all turns out to be nothing, you'll probably never get any compensation for these false allegations, so your out the money.

Moreover, the only justice you could get would be to prosecute the stewardess for making a false police report, which is a felony, and hopefully get her some jail time. But most often then not the prosecutor and judge won't go along with that."

"So what am I to do?" John stated despondently.

"John," I stated, "a couple weeks ago I ran a case in Ohio where a judge and his wife were baby-sitting a newborn female child for some wealthy friends of his. The baby-sitting detail went uneventful until the kid went home with her parents. The parents happened to notice a rash on the child's inner thigh and crotch area and therefore assumed and suspected that the judge had sexually abused their daughter.

Now the judge, whom I have done work for in the past called me in and was totally at a loss on what to do and appeared to be having a nervous breakdown. He stated, "Frank, I don't know what to do and I see my whole life and career passing in front of me and even as a judge, I am helpless.

Here, my wife and I do a good deed for friends of mine during a trying period of their life and now I am looked upon as a pervert or child molester…. my career is ruined…please help me, Frank."

Anyway, to the quick the judge passed with flying colors and got his life back on track and will be able to complete his tenure as judge on the bench without any negative feedback.

His case has similarities like yours, John, because like him you want to cut off the head of Medusa before things get out of control. Am I correct John?"

"Yes sir, that is correct, that's exactly how I feel." John stated.

"So, step one John, is to tell the truth to what happened, if your ready," asked Tracy.

"I'm ready," John stated.

Tracy replied, "As I understand it John, you are an Air Transport Pilot and instructor with about 12,000 flying hours and your base of operations is Chicago O'Hare International. You are 41 years old and have no physical or mental liabilities that could affect the outcome of your polygraph examination today, is that correct?"

"That is correct," John, stated, "last May, I departed in the evening from Detroit Metropolitan Airport for Chicago. We landed the 727 aircraft at Chicago O'Hare and the flight up until then was totally uneventful as the passengers were departing the scene. As all the passengers departed the plane, I told the engineer co-pilot to secure certain equipment that we had on board for our corporate extension office. After he gathered the equipment and manifest list he left for our extension office and would wait up for me to have dinner in about an hour. At this time, the co-pilot departed the aircraft, and I was left with Paula, the stewardess, and her young seven-year-old daughter Amanda."

"Okay," Tracy stated.

"At this time", John stated, "Paula left for the bathroom to freshen up and asked if I would watch Amanda. So I complied and said I would."

"Okay," Tracy stated.

As John continued, "Well, when Paula returned from the restroom about five minutes later, Amanda then stated she had to go to the bathroom. So Paula accompanied Amanda to the bathroom for whatever reason.

I then heard a ruckus in the bathroom, which sounded like Amanda was crying. A short time later Paula and Amanda exited the bathroom and I get this cold dead stare from Paula.

So being concerned and thinking Amanda had a medical problem I asked Paula if there was something wrong."

"We're listening," I stated.

"Well, Paula yells at me and states, "How could you?" and I responded, "How could I what?"

Paula then states that Amanda claimed that I grabbed her breast and buttocks while she, Paula, was in the bathroom.

First I thought it was a joke but within seconds I realized I had just entered into the realm of the *twilight zone* and that my integrity, which took a lifetime to build, had been compromised.

So when I approached Amanda to question her, Paula yelled at me and stated to get away from her. Then Paula called me a pervert and exited the plane with Amanda stating that she was going to our corporate extension office and report me.

Needless to say, I was stunned and dumbfounded. I still am.

Then within minutes, the corporate phone rang in the plane and the corporate extension manager and a stewardess union representative wanted to talk to me about an incident.

As they say the rest is history and I was instructed to get an attorney as soon as possible to discuss my options and defense.

When I tried to explain this to my wife, though she supports me, she gave me this strange look like she married a pervert or something."

"The look like…. how could you?" Tracy asked.

"Ya," John answered as he looked down at the floor.

"Well, John, did you do it?" I asked.

"Hell, no." John angrily yelled back.

Tracy asked, "John have you ever been accused of something you did not do?"

John answered spontaneously, "Yes, right now."

"This event in question?" Tracy asked.

"Yes…this event." John stated.

"Good answer John." I stated.

"Pardon me?" as John looked at me inquisitively.

"Oh nothing, John." as I looked into his eyes.

Tracy then asked John, "Have you ever read any polygraph manuals on how to allegedly beat the polygraph examination that are for sale on the Internet by examiners who have sold their soul to the dark side?"

"No, why should I?", John stated.

"Because if you had John, you better tell us now, because it is indicative of deception if you had.  Moreover, we will fail you if we detect your lying or if we recognize any countermeasures that may be applied from these ill constructed manuals", I stated.

"Why would I do that?" John again asked inquisitively.

Tracy came back, "Because *uniformed* people who are *desperate* will buy that garbage or believe in that garbage in an attempt to defeat the polygraph examination. And garbage it is!"

"Then why are you concerned?" John queried.

"We're not…but it's a warning…. because if you had then we encourage you to walk out of the examination room right now. You see John we know their garbage doesn't work and they are only selling this material because they sold their soul to the dark side for blood money.

Moreover, the numerous people we had failed had found out the hard way after the examination, that is, they thought they had an advantage over us but sadly found out they been had and we played them into our hands", I stated.

"Okay, that's fine, I have nothing to hide. Further, I never took a polygraph examination before and nor did I look up alleged countermeasures on the Internet." John stated.

"Fine, then lets continue, John. The polygraph is 85% to 95% accurate based on research. We are not going to get into a long useless debate on what your friends may or may not have said about the polygraph or alleged ways to beat the test.

So, today we are going to be monitoring certain parameters in your body that you can't control. Specifically, we will be monitoring certain changes in your heart, sweat glands and breathing. You will be given a battery of tests, on average somewhere between two to six tests, where each test takes approximately five minutes with an interval in-between. During the testing phase, all we want from you is to remain calm with your feet flat on the floor, palms down and eyes closed. There will be no unnecessary moving or talking and whatever you do, do naturally. You will be answering all questions with a simple yes or no. Some tests we will make you deliberately lie and other tests you will answer the questions silently in your mind and not verbally.

Further, in order to pass your examination it is irrelevant if we like each other or not for it has no bearing on the final outcome. Figuratively speaking, we are not two gladiators in the coliseum of life fighting against each other. Moreover, this examination is not you against *the box*, that is, you against the polygraph instrument as if it were Robocop or something. But rather it is you against yourself and the only way your going to pass is by telling the absolute and complete truth about everything, understand?", Tracy stated.

"Yes, I understand but I have a question or two, if I may ask?" John inquired.

"Sure." I stated, "Fire away."

"Well I know you people are professionals and have explained everything in great detail to me, but as a pilot, I know pilots make mistakes from time to time. I mean we are only human and even though you mentioned the validity of the examination percentage wise, is there any way that an innocent person can fail? I mean when I fly planes my passengers trust me, yet I know that anytime a person enters an aircraft the potential for a mistake exists.

So, have any of you ever failed an innocent person?", Asked John.

I interjected, "John you are talking about *false positives* and *false negatives. False positive* is when an innocent or truthful person has been found deceptive. *False negative* is when a deceptive person has been found truthful.

In Tracy's and my career, neither one of us has ever failed a truthful person, which is false positive. *For our prime directive is simple, which is to exonerate and clear the captive innocent.*

Now regarding, false negatives, that is, where a deceptive examinee was found innocent. My answer would be perhaps I have over my thirty some years of running examinations.

The reason being, is that if I error, like you, I error on the side of caution.

For as we say in police work, *it is better to let ten guilty men go free then it is to incarcerate an innocent person.*

Even though the *polygraph technique* is not infallible, it is nevertheless a highly accurate investigative tool. For it has numerous safeguards built in to protect the innocent yet despite that I take it to a higher level based on my comprehensive police and private eye background that most polygraph examiners don't have.

So, hopefully I answered your question, that you flying with your 12,000 hours in high performance aircraft and me with thousands of criminal polygraph tests under my belt, both of us are human and still subject to error. Good enough?"

"Good enough, I am ready for testing," John stated smiling.

I came back and stated, "John, the test started the moment I laid eyes on you. For, attitude, subtle indicators, spontaneous admissions, body language, demeanor, consistency and believability of your storyline are all critical parts of the polygraph examination and not just the polygraph charts."

"I hear you." John replied.

I then stated, "John, let me asked you a question off the record, seeing that flying was once dear to my heart? Is the flying business still good?", I asked John inquisitively.

"Ahhh.," John hesitated, "if I had to do it again, I wouldn't do it. I miss my wife and my three kids for I am gone four days a week without seeing them. I'm an electrical engineer by trade; I should have gone that way in hindsight. I am a family man and I would have been home more if I went the engineering route instead of aviation."

"Interesting, I've heard that a few times throughout my life. Yet, even now I wonder if I was just unfortunate, that is, at the wrong place and wrong time or someone upstairs was looking out for me. I guess, I'll never know", as I looked out the window with a thousand yard stare.

Tracy got us back on track by asking John, "What do you know about the stewardess Paula, John?"

John replied, "Paula has told her fellow stewardess that she had been raped by her father as a young girl and that she had been married two or three times before. What I understand is, she is a single mother trying to make ends meet on stewardess wages…which isn't much."

"Has she ever told you she liked you or loved you or wanted to spend some time with you?" Tracy inquired.

John laughed, "Ahh…I always felt she kind of liked me but I didn't press the issue. She really wasn't my kind of woman anyway."

I stated, "Hmmm…didn't have the seven year itch John for some strange?"

John laughed, "No, my wife and I have a good relationship."

Tracy laughing, "Then why would she set you up, John? Money?"

John responded, "I don't have any money, she came to the wrong guy if she thought I had money. Hell, I believe she perhaps just wanted some leave of absence from work and blamed it on me."

Tracy asked, "You mean like sexual harassment?"

John responded, "I don't know if it would be sexual harassment but perhaps a hostile work environment or something like that."

"You mean like all this is leading up to a force quit and a settlement out of court and you're the bag man?" I shot back.

"Yaa...something like that. If this wasn't so serious, it would be funny." John stated.

I looked at John and said, "Yes, it could be serious John, you most probably have a second degree criminal sexual conduct charge heading your way which could be a five to fifteen year jail rap in the big house."

"That's not good," John said grimly.

I stated, "Okay John here are the questions that I will be asking you, so answer them with a yes or no."

"Okay." John affirmed.

"Your first question then John is this:

"On the date and time in question did you touch Amanda's breast?"

"No."

"On the date and time in question did you touch Amanda's buttocks?"

"No."

"Are the allegations Paula stated about you fondling Amanda true?"

"No."

"Have you ever touched Amanda at anytime for sexual gratification?"

"No."

"Have you lied to the polygraph examiner in any way to give yourself an alibi in this case?"

"No"

"Have you ever fondled any child in your life for sexual gratification?"

"No."

"Now seeing that this is a polygraph examination John and that you are taking this examination on your own volition, I have to believe that you are not a liar or a sexual pervert. Am I correct?"

"Yes," answered John with a confused look.

Tracy then jumped in and stated, "Good, we are glad to hear that. That said; let me ask you this John:

Not connected with this case have you ever engaged in any unusual sexual activity?"

"Ahhh.... you mean like with my wife?", John queried.

I said, "Are you a pervert John?"

"No, but I am not sure I understand the question." John looked at me confused.

Tracy then stated without waiting or qualifying the question, "Well if your not a sexual pervert, then what's your answer.

John looked at Tracy and stated, "My answer is no, but I am not sure what unusual sexual activity means."

Tracy then stated, "John another question I want to ask you is this, but remember you fail your examination if you're a liar."

"Okay," John stated.

Tracy looked at John and said, "Not connected with this case have you ever told an important lie to someone who trusted you?"

"Damn, important lie? Wow, that's a tough one...whats important?" John inquisitively asked.

I jumped in and stated, "You tell me John, are you a liar?"

"No," John stated.

"Well," Tracy stated again without qualifying the question, "then John, what is your answer?"

"I guess no...but I have to say those last two questions bothered me."

I stated to John, "Until now have you told us the absolute and complete truth about everything to the best of your knowledge and belief?"

"Yes, I have," John stated.

"Do you accept those questions John and are you ready for testing," Tracy asked.

"Yes, I am Tracy," stated John.

As I sat back in my chair and watched Tracy "*hook up*" John, I continued to watch his body language for any signs of deception.

During the testing phase, Tracy handed me back the charts for review as she figuratively continued to pound away at John for any signs of inconsistencies in his story line.

When the examination was concluded, Tracy asked John, if any of the questions bothered him. He stated the questions about an important lie and unusual sexual activity seemed to bother him, for he wasn't sure how to answered them.

This to me, after looking over the charts was an indication that the control questions had a grip on him, which was what we hoped to see and hear.

When all was said and done, Tracy and I reviewed the charts as John looked on wondering if his lifestyle had come to a crashing halt or if he would go free.

As I looked at him I could imagine how he wondered if he would stay up in fame or come crashing down in flames without a parachute. For he feared something that I knew long ago and that is caging a bird of paradise.

*I knew from experience that ones destiny whether good or bad hangs on such slender threads, as this. Indeed, I knew it all to well.*

At this time Tracy, after conferring with me, stated to John as he awaited his fate that his polygrams based on the case facts available revealed no consistent specific responses indicative of deception, thereby passing his examination.

I could only marvel on the look on John's face in that one microsecond of time as it transformed from shear apprehension to a tranquil state of peace. I compared it to the conversion of Mary Magdalene when she repented from her state of sin to belief in Jesus Christ in the twinkling of an eye.

As John got up I could see his eyes were watery as he hugged Tracy and thanked her. A total sigh of relief was upon his face as he looked straight into my eyes and also thanked me.

As he walked out of the office, I said to myself, "Alls well that ends well" and I let it go like that.

I instructed Tracy to call in the report to the Luna Pier office and dictate it to Coco, as I walked out of the conference room to see how Kelly was doing.

## *Chapter 7 - The Tune up Man*

As I walked into Kelly's conference room where she was attempting to conduct a polygraph examination, I notice the examinee, a twenty-year-old white male banging a tuning fork on the table.

I asked him what was the purpose of that and he stated he was a music major and the sound of the tuning fork calmed his nerves.

So I walked up to the young man and took the tuning fork out of his hand. I then stated to him, "Look, friend, your attorney down the hall feels you need to take a polygraph examination for criminal sexual conduct in the first degree. Do you want it yes or no?"

The examinee didn't say anything.

I asked, "Kelly, what is this examinees name?"

"Frank," Kelly responded, "His first name is Mitch."

"Okay, listen up Mitch, I am going to ask you one more time, do you want the examination or not? It's your call pal, either way is fine with me."

Mitch hesitated as if he wanted to say something and then stopped.

Picking up on this, I stated to Mitch, "Mitch a confession or an admission to the crime at hand is a polygraph examination. Why don't you save us all a lot of trouble and get this matter that's bothering you off your chest."

Mitch still said nothing.

I asked Kelly who the plaintiff was and she stated the mother of the thirteen year old girl named Shirley, who claims her daughter, was raped at Mitch's apartment.

"Mitch," Kelly asked. "Has your attorney told you the severity of your charges and what can happen to you if these charges are found to true?"

Mitch while gazing at Kelly's beauty stated, "He mentioned I could be in trouble."

"A thirteen year old girl? That's putting it mildly, Mitch!" I yelled back. "I think you may want to wake up now and level with us, otherwise you can have it your way and face the prosecutors course of action."

"Shirley lied," stated Mitch.

"Listen Mitch," I stated. "It's better we know the circumstances, so we can inform your attorney of your circumstances. In order for your attorney to build an appropriate defense for you...i.e., save your ass."

Mitch looking down at the floor raised his head and stated, "My father and my attorney Mr. Cabman are good friends and elders in our church.

Shirley and I at times sang in the choir and that's how I got to know her."

"Okay," Kelly stated. "Go on."

"Promise you won't tell my father or Mr. Cabman?" Mitch asked.

I turned away, for I don't compromise with rapists or potential rapists but sweet-heart Kelly took the bait.

"Consider it done Mitch," Kelly stated.

"Well," Mitch stated. "About three weeks ago after church, I asked Shirley if she wanted to go to my apartment to show her my new guitar. Her mother who sang in the quire with us didn't think it was appropriate so stated no, that is, not without her presence.

"That's reasonable," I stated.

"Well," Mitch continued, "Shirley insisted and started getting emotional by saying she was big enough to go alone and didn't need her mother. Finally her mother gave in and stated to Shirley that she can go but has to be home before dark. Shirley agreed."

As I am waiting for the punch line now, Mitch continued.

"At my apartment, I showed Shirley my guitar which she liked. So I played a few tunes on it then let her have a try. After about an hour we stopped playing the guitar so Shirley and I sat on my couch and started to watch television. At this time Shirley asked if I had anything to drink because she was thirsty, so I went to the refrigerator to get her a pop. I then poured her pop in a cup and dropped in two sleeping pills."

Immediately Kelly became aggressive with Mitch by taking it personally, though she was trained to never breakup an admission or confession until the examinee's finished their testimony.

"Why did you do that?" Kelly asked.

"Ahh, at first I just wanted to see if she could taste the difference in the pop," Mitch stated. "Then after about a half hour she started getting groggy and fell asleep on my couch."

"Come on, Mitch, that's not the real reason, how could you do something like that?" Kelly yelled angrily.

As Kelly continued getting loud and angry with Mitch, I had to override her, otherwise we could lose the confession or other key elements to the crime.

"Hold on Kelly, sit back, will you," as I looked at Kelly. "Continue Mitch with your story, you stated she was asleep on your couch. What happened next?"

Kelly looked at me and was upset that I stepped on her. For a moment I thought she was going to leave the room after telling me first to go to hell or some other place where the sun doesn't shine.

When Mitch realized he wasn't going to get hit by the wrath of Kelly, he continued his story.

"When I shook Shirley, she remained asleep, so I kissed her a couple times on the lips as if we were making love.

So then I lifted her dress up to her stomach.

When she still didn't wake up I unzipped my pant's zipper and pulled out my dick and masturbated by rubbing my dick against her legs. Yet, she still didn't wake up.

So I tried to put my dick in her mouth while she was asleep as if she was giving me a blow job."

"Continue," I stated.

"Her mouth was closed and I couldn't get my dick in her mouth, so I pulled down her pants and tried to stick my dick in her vagina, but I couldn't get it in.

Finally I got so frustrated and mad that I couldn't cum in her mouth or screw her that I pulled that tuning fork you're holding out of my pocket and pushed it up her vagina as hard as I could."

As I looked at this sick puppy, I laid down the tuning fork on the table and stated, "Continue Mitch."

"I just kept jamming it up her vagina over and over again until she started bleeding. But she still didn't wake up, so I got scared.

I began to shake her real hard but she still wouldn't wake up, so I called for an ambulance. When the ambulance came I told them I found her in my apartment drugged and crazy and she did this to herself. They then took her by ambulance to the hospital.

Afterwards I got scared and left the apartment when the ambulance took Shirley away."

"That's it?" Kelly stated.

Mitch continued, "The hospital called her mother and stated that her daughter had been raped. Her mother insisted that I was the only one who could have done it.

I told my parents that Shirley just went crazy and fingered herself because I would not have sex with her. They wouldn't tell Shirley's mother and father of this."

"At the time the ambulance came Mitch, did any police officers arrive at the scene or were summoned?" I asked.

"No, they didn't come or were asked, as far as I could tell." Mitch stated. "But later they came and talked to my parents, who got me Attorney Cabman."

"Mitch, the police didn't take you in for questioning?" I curiously asked.

"No, they didn't," stated Mitch.

"Damn…how can this be?" As I shook my head, I found it hard to believe.

Kelly stated, "Mitch, you can leave now for your attorneys office and notify him that we are done."

"I'm free to leave?" as if he was asking for verification.

"Yes, you can go, Mitch," I restated.

As Mitch left the office, Kelly looked at me and asked how could I have held back from shooting him with my police revolver.

I couldn't answer that professionally, so I said nothing.

Mr. Cabman came into the conference room, rubbing his hands with a look on his face, real or pretend, as if he had been expecting his client to have passed.

"How'd he do?" Mr. Cabman asked with great expectation.

So, Kelly and I told Mr. Cabman the story, as told to us. Surprisingly, Mr. Cabman sat down as if shocked with the look like he was just told that he had terminal cancer.

We told him that Mitch had confessed to the crime and we gave him our negative diagnostic opinion.

Mr. Cabman stated, "Mitch is a good kid and his father is a long time dear friend of mine. I don't know how I'm going to tell him this?"

Kelly and I both shook our heads not knowing either.

"Mr. Legion, I would appreciate that no report be sent to me. Further if his father should ask you about this matter, refer him to me…damn, I actually believed Mitch was clean."

"Well," I said. "Mr. Cabman the audio tapes are available if you want to hear them for yourself and by the way here's his tuning fork."

"Man oh man," Mr. Cabman looking at me troubled, "I don't know how Mitch's, father is going to handle this. Hell, it could kill him.

Damn, I'm glad you weren't a public examiner, a warrant would be issued now and he would ultimately be sent away for life."

Mr. Cabman left the room presumably to inform Mitch's father on the situation.

I looked at Kelly and she apparently had the same thought I had. That Mitch was going up the river for a very long time or to a psychiatric ward for the same duration.

## *Chapter 8 - Tit for Tat*

As Kelly and I completed the examination on Mitch, Mr. Cabman's secretary came in and informed us that my next case, an anonymous high-powered client would appreciate it if I ran the polygraph examination at his location tomorrow.

The secretary further stated another anonymous client in the same general area wanted an examination of which would be discussed at the scene.

The secretary wanted to know if I would agree to this on such a short notice. She stated it was about a half hour drive to the state capitol building, in Indianapolis. After thinking about it for a while and wondering what was the deal with all this cloak and dagger stuff, I reluctantly agreed and informed her that I would do them tomorrow.

That said, the girls and I took the rest of the day off to shop and catch up on paperwork.

The following day I drove to Indianapolis and after showing my credentials to security I was escorted to a room full of American flags with political plaques on the wall. I didn't know who all the political figures were on the wall for I was not from Indiana, but it stated senators, representatives and governors, which indicated to me that my client was immersed in politics. As I sat there for about five minutes looking at the beautiful wooden floor and the surrounding décor, I could not help but marvel how well things were made in days gone by.

A short time later I heard noise from one of the side rooms and two professional well-groomed young men emerged dressed in expensive suits and introduced themselves as only political consultants, but they would not tell me their names.

Throughout my career I have ran into numerous John Does who for one reason or another wanted to remain anonymous. I would play their game for a while but by the end of the day I would know who they were, why they wanted a test and what they were afraid of revealing to me.

In cases like this, examinees would take the polygraph examination and assuming they passed would show the report to any concerned parties in question without revealing their identity or concerned parties to the examiner.

Apparently, these John and Jane Does did not realize that we examiners do not put our signatures on any forms without knowingly identifying all concerned parties in question.

It was like a game with some male examinees who would play up to you as if you were their long lost buddies from Outer Mongolia. They would go as far as offering you drinks and promises to take you out on their boat with lady escorts. They would literally throw money at your feet and treat you like a homecoming king but their motives were obvious.

While some female examinees would expose as much cleavage to you as possible without having it fall out of their bra then compliment their breasts with a long and silky exposed shank of leg. The kicker was when they tried to seduce you with their smiling eyes and voluptuous lips. They would look at you when the examination was completed and in a tender loving voice just before they heard their dismal results, they would say softly "Can we work it off?"

As we sat down these alleged political consultants sized me up and looked me overhead to toe as I awaited their opening move.

Political consultant number one stated, "Mr. Legion, we have a problem and we need it to be resolved in the most discrete manner and as soon as possible."

"Okay," I stated, "but I am going to need to know who you are and your associates name at least on a first name basis.

By the way you can call me Frank."

Political consultant number one stated, "We apologize for our evasiveness Frank, but in our line of business discretion is always a primary concern.

You may call me Sydney and my associate's name is Harry."

"Okay," I stated. "It is a pleasure again to meet you Sydney and Harry."

"The pleasure is ours most assuredly, Frank," answered Sydney.

"I noticed there are a lot of American flags in this room. Is this case military related?" I queried.

Harry responded, "No, but regarding the flags…Ahhh…yes, I am a Captain in the U.S. Army Reserves."

"Oh," As I extended my hand for a handshake. "Well Harry, Captain Legion, United States Marine Corps."

"Oh yah, I'll be damned," Harry stated as he shook my hand. "Did you go through Quantico?"

"Indeed, Quantico and The Basic School," I replied proudly.

"I'll be damned," Harry stated again. "I've been in fourteen years."

"Oh, really, wow. I was in a total of five years, I loved the military life and I wanted to stay in the Marine Corps, but as they say, life got in my way," I replied laughing.

Harry laughed, as Sydney left to address a question from their secretary.

I looked at Harry and stated, "Okay Harry, I run the polygraph examination by the numbers and everything will be explained beforehand. Furthermore, I speak loud because I was a former high explosive bomb technician and I have a high frequency hearing loss."

Harry's face lightened up then stated, "Oh, I am also a high explosive bomb technician. I trained with Egyptian bomb technicians for nine months and was a liaison officer with the Egyptian Special Forces."

"That's impressive, isn't that something," I stated. "I trained with Navy Seals, C.I.A., Israeli's and the New York Bomb Squad, et al."

"Wow, that's also impressive, I am curious, who did you find to be the best?" Harry asked.

"Well, Harry they were all excellent but I was most impressed with the Navy Seals Underwater Demolition Team, then the New York Bomb Squad. I could hold my own against other U.S. agencies including the C.I.A. and Israeli's.

You would think the Israeli's would be the best, according to our controlled mainstream media, but they weren't. Americans were more intelligent and better focused. To the best of my knowledge and belief Americans beat the Israeli's hands down."

Harry looked dumbfounded, "Huh, that's surprising, one would think, with all the bombings over there in Israel they would be real good.

The Egyptians, I trained with were excellent and I learned a lot from them."

I stated, "The Egyptians have to be good with all their internal sects and religious extremists within their country.

Anyway, if I were in a pinch, I would take Army and Navy trained demolition experts any day over foreigners."

Harry looked at the ceiling and stated. "Well seeing that we are both bomb technicians from different branches of services, which is a rarity, would you mind if I digress for a moment and ask you what do you think about so many conflicting bomb stories I hear and certain alleged acts of terrorism?"

"Shoot, go ahead Harry", I responded.

"In brief, what's your take on the Lockerbie bombing, Oklahoma bombing, the 1993 World Trade Center attack and 911", Harry asked.

"Are you asking my professional opinion as one bomb technician to another and strictly off the record?" I asked smirking.

"Why of course", Harry stated.

"Well, Lockerbie, I was directly or indirectly involved in depending on ones interpretation of the data.

The Central Intelligence Agency, prior to Lockerbie, and according to a newspaper article ran on the front page of, "The Wall Street Gazette", and also C.I.A. personnel who told me first hand that their intelligence agencies could not penetrate the tight-lipped Arab community anywhere in the United States.

The C.I.A. needed patriotic Americans that they could trust and were "on the inside" to help them build an American spy ring from Dearborn, Michigan to Lebanon. Moreover, they needed American patriots and American military veterans who shall I say were "on the inside" of the largest Arab community in North America.

As with any American patriot, when I was approached and courted, I was willing to help my country in an attempt to turn the tide against terrorism and communist infiltrators that were cropping up within the Arab community from time to time.

So I initiated contacts, in secret, with patriots, who were American veterans and political activists within the Arab community. In a short period of time all those individuals I contacted were all willing to assist and a spy ring was built from Dearborn, Michigan to Lebanon. But as time passed, I started to have second thoughts when my experience, intelligence and my police officers six sense kicked in. I mysteriously began recovering electronic explosive devices during my tour of duty in the Dearborn South End, which led me to believe that Arabs were not constructing these explosive devices but rather a foreign Middle Eastern power that had all to gain by vilifying the Arab people. I knew I was being played especially after I rendered safe alleged explosive devices that would appear on local the television channels. All the while it was implied that Arab terrorists working within our borders, which alarmed Americans, designed these explosive devices. Flags started going up and I knew that the C.I.A. in conjunction with dual card holding foreign agents were now playing the Arab community just like they had played other American ethnic groups.

I felt betrayed and realized that the C.I.A. at its highest level was not a intelligent agency for the people of the United States of America but rather an intelligence gathering agency working for, "The Powers That Be", known as the global elite in order to maintain their status quo on power.

So, I informed my contacts of my distrust of our operation and informed them that our patriotism and love of country was being played against us and our work was not for Americans, or America, but rather for "The Powers That Be."

I now felt and believed that the upper echelons of the Central Intelligence Agency were acting only in the best interest of corporate America, our military industrial complex, international bankers, the Saudi Arabian hierarchy and the Queen of England.

So, I told my contacts of my second thoughts and much to my surprise they felt similar and were very concerned. I wished my associates the best of luck and advised them that I was getting out and for each of them to follow their own conscience.

Without further adieu, Lockerbie occurred and the blame initially was put on Arab terrorists out of Libya who allegedly filled a radio with explosives that supposedly belonged to a young kid who lived in Dearborn, Michigan. The intelligence agencies attempted to blame him for collaborating with Libyan Arab terrorists who exploded a Pan Am, Boeing 747, *Clipper Maid of the Seas*" over Lockerbie, Scotland, in which 243 people died along with 16 crew members and 11 people on the ground. Pan Am's final destination was Detroit Metropolitan Airport; a stone throw from Dearborn, Michigan.

Of course the young mans father denied his sons involvement and he was correct. Yet, the intelligence agencies and Zionist controlled mainstream media continued to vilify him and seeded the American public and the world with propaganda that Arabs sponsored terrorism. The intelligent agencies inferred directly that these *GOD fearing people known as Arabs* were terrorists and were not only spawning within America's borders but also hiding within every crack and crevice.

When I read the morning paper regarding the Lockerbie bombing investigation it confirmed my suspicions that this was an intelligence operations and the story line as told by our government to the American people was a total sham. By extrapolation I realized that the Arab people were not the primary target, though falsely vilified.

*But rather, Lockerbie and up to 911 was a plan devised by wicked men who deliberately intended to mislead and win the support of the American people as a prelude to war* **whose strategic objective was oil**.

So to answer your question Harry, the C.I.A. and Mossad (Israeli intelligence) did Lockerbie and Colonel Muammar Gaddafi of Libya was set up to take the fall.

The real culprits are in Washington D.C. and in Israel, though I do not exclude MI-6 of England.

"Sounds like you don't have much faith in the C.I.A. and Israel," Harry shot back.

"No, not really, it is my belief that the middle and lower echelon agents of the C.I.A. are American patriots, like you and me. However, the upper class of this agency, I believe beyond a reasonable doubt are demonic and serve the dark side.

As far as the state of Israel goes, by definition under the R.I.C.C.O. statue, it is a crime syndicate controlled by *"want to be"* Semitic people who are Asiatic Mongoloid-Turks that bedded down with the Semitic Jews somewhere in the past. Moreover to be a Jew is not a nationality but a religion.

*"What better place to hide Satan's children but among God's people!*

The God fearing Semitic Jews in Israel are facing the same dilemma that God fearing Americans and the world's people as a whole are condemned to, that is, we are slaves to these *"fallen angels"* who rule and control over us.

These angels in human form, *Satan's own*, use our daughters for exploitation and for their meat. Then, this same power, use our sons to step on land mines and to murder peasants whose only crimes were that they were born over oil.

Jesus Christ, declared two thousand years ago that Israeli's temple was a synagogue of Satan. If this is so, then what must be the moral compass of its patrons and the fruit of their work?

While our temple, St. Paul's Cathedral at the Vatican, *"the smoke of Satan"* has entered the sacred sanctuary in June 1963 where a *black mass* was conducted to *enthrone Lucifer*.

The Vatican has become in effect an enclave for perverted pedophiles and homosexual men.

Pope John XXIII, due to geopolitics, refused to honor the mandate of heaven, by the Virgin Mary, which pertained to the third secret of Fatima and every subsequent Pope thereafter had also failed to honor her request even though some belonged to her religious order. Because of these popes horrific decisions and inactions they are likened to the Pharisees of the synagogue "do as they say but not as they do." For they sit upon the chair of Peter and place heavy burdens upon men by telling them how they should come to Jesus Christ and love Mary, the Queen of Heaven. Yet these same popes when given the third secret of Fatima by the Queen of Heaven to alleviate the suffering of mankind if certain conditions are met, they refuse to honor it.

When Pope John XXIII refused to honor the third secret mandated by the Queen of Heaven in 1960 or protect his church which is upon this rock that over one billion people religiously adhere to and where not even the gates of hell shall prevail against it, it fell out of grace.

It follows therefore, that in 1963 under the reign of Pope Paul VI, Lucifer was enthroned within the cathedral of St. Paul during a black mass. Now the Shepard has been struck and the sheep have been scattered and the whole human species has entered into a period of chastisement and suffering.

*How deep must Hell be for these people to hide their shame!*

As far as the Oklahoma bombing goes, it was an inside job by the United States government as far as I know, "The Powers That Be" had extreme concern regarding the rising tide of the states militias who were fed up with the encroachment and enslavement of the federal government who were protecting the criminal bankers of the Federal Reserve. So they, the government, staged a diversionary explosion and blamed it on the state militias, which forced them to go into hiding.

Moreover, information provided to me from people who were explosive bomb technicians and certain high individuals involved in the aftermath of the explosion in Oklahoma informed me of this also.

I vividly remember a piece of information given to me from someone "in the know" about the Oklahoma bombing that stood out above the rest. It was after the explosion where a human leg was found contained within a U.S. military uniform. The leg apparently belonged to a black female and when certain authorities discovered it instead of giving it a proper military burial decided to just throw it back into the heap of debris for disposal or to be eaten by the birds."

I looked at Harry's troubled face while he shook his head.

"Damn," Harry stated, still shaking his head. "It gets you to wonder doesn't it?"

"Yes it does, I mean it's not the slithering bankers kid's leg but probably some single black women trying to make a better life for her family by trying to get out of the ghetto."

Being a military man, Harry's face still looked troubled.

Then Harry stated, "I don't know what to make of what you just said but it is distressing to say the least."

"Is it what I just said Harry, which many think is pure bullshit or does it have a ring of truth? But then again maybe you taking this polygraph examination with me and possibly being thrown into the heap concerns you?" I said laughing.

Harry also started laughing, but with a hint of desperation in his voice, "No, it is not your qualification as a polygraph examiner you came recommended but rather my concern of how and if my career will be affected."

"I've been aware from the beginning that I came recommended, Harry," smiling as Harry looked at me.

As far as the 1993 bombing of the World Trade Center, certain bomb technicians who were at the scene stated to me, first hand, how they were told to search, where to search and what to look for and *when*…by the F.B.I.

As you know Harry at any bomb scene, bomb technicians take charge of the scene and the paper pusher's stand at a distance, but in this case, the search was controlled.

Mossad and the United States intelligent agencies failed to drop the World Trade Center at that time, but despite that they had their duped Arab patsies in place to take the fall for the home team.

In any case, our **government leaders** on that day were treasonous and cowardly and should have been tried for the murder of 3,000 innocent Americans who died that day.

This C.I.A. and Mossad operation supported by corrupted politicians duped, hoodwinked, snookered and bamboozled the American people into wars that had nothing to do with terrorists but rather it had to do with colonialism, hegemony and seizing the resources of oil rich nations.

At the time, numerous Israeli agents were captured malingering around our federal buildings with maps and diagrams only to be arrested. They were polygraphed and they failed, but still they were released and sent back to Israel per our treasonous leaders and dual cardholders who were planted in critical positions of authority.

The Pentagon was hit by a modified cruise missile disguised as an airplane while thermite, which produces a great amount of heat, was placed in World Trade Center building prior to the explosion.

Furthermore, Flight 93 which crashed in Pennsylvania was shot down by American made F-16 Falcons, flown by American pilots, using heat seeking missiles. These pilots belonged to the North Dakota Air National Guard.

The planes that hit the World Trade Center is believed to have been radio controlled by the United States Space Command who may have even used bunker busters on the World Trade Center.

All the time President Bush was reading a book about a *goat,* not a lamb mind you, but a goat to little children in Florida, while Vice President Cheney, the draft dodger, barricaded himself in his underground bunker.

*All the while American women in shredded dresses were jumping from the World Trade Center fifty stories up or more on fire............AND THE FIVE ISRAELI'S DANCED!*

Then Larry Silverjudas, owner of one of the building complex's and a duel cardholder and suspected pagan Mossad stooge, used bomb technician terminology to initiate an explosive firing train by saying **"pull it"** on World Trade Center Building Number Seven.

The explosive charges that were already in place by foreign agents exploded and the building collapsed on itself *without even being touched.*

Then the American people march off to war and unknowingly murder 1,000,000 innocent Arab peasants who had nothing to do with 911.

But the highlight of all this is when these same Americans come home and genuflect before Jesus Christ in church as if they went about doing their heavenly fathers business.

Why doesn't Jesus come and Rapture us, they say, we're beautiful children though we never questioned the governments unbelievable story or refused to carry out an immoral or unethical order to murder?"

Kingdoms cannot change Harry, until the hearts of men change!"

Harry looked at me confused…. but said nothing. Though I knew he was hurting inside like me as with all American veterans who had finally woke up to the sober reality that "We the People" are being used as dumb animals and suckers to advance the agenda of the Illuminati or it's derivative name the Skull and Bones.

Regrettably Harry, I too in my youth was that same sucker and dumb animal that trusted my leaders without question. For I to once had a sparkle in my eye with young men's dreams only to have them extinguished by wicked men.

Am I babbling too much Harry or is it getting to hot in the kitchen? You asked me so I told you what I know, what you do with that information is up to you.

**But then again I'm a chronic liar and the government version of 911 is the correct version.**

You see Harry, it isn't important whether you believe what I just said or consider me a conspiracy nut. To me the only importance is that I know the truth to the best of my knowledge and belief by applying my observation, common sense, intelligence and the talents that GOD gave me.

That said now, where was I.

Oh yes, I have a question for you, Harry, are you being charged criminally or is this a civil matter?"

Harry hesitated, still numb from my reply stated, "At this time it is a civil matter and hopefully it will not end up criminally."

"So," I asked. "You don't anticipate taking a public examination at any police department or state police post do you?"

"Not at this time …and I hope not," Harry stated with a concerned tone.

As I looked over Harry's worried face, I asked, "So then this is a preemptive strike on your behalf to test the waters of the polygraph technique and hopefully cut-off the head of the Medusa before it strikes, is this correct?"

"Well….ahhh…yes," Harry stated.

"That's what I figured Harry.

But I want to advise you that a private investigative unit I have in my briefcase has signaled me that there is a remote security camera on the wall behind me, which is functioning and directly focused on us.

Technically speaking, that is not allowed during a polygraph session at anytime except in special cases or for a public examiner. Just so you know if your case goes before a public examiner, your own attorney will not be allowed to be present during the polygraph examination.

For now Harry, you can leave that camera on until the testing phase begins."

"Thank you," Harry stated.

At this time Sydney walked back into the room and stated, "I'm sorry I had to attend to an emergency matter. I just advised our secretary that we are not to be disturbed, henceforth."

"Good," I said. As I watched Sydney sit close to Harry's chair as if he was a defense attorney.

"I have to asked you now Harry and Sydney, just who you really are and what is your function in this capitol building?"

Harry and Sydney looked at each other. Then Sydney gave Harry an affirmative nod.

Harry looked at me as if resigned to his fate and stated, "I am the state house of representatives majority whip."

"Oh dear, no wonder your concerned, Harry. Am I about to open up a can of worms for you and will the press be waiting outside this door when I'm done?"

"I hope not Frank."

"So you are a member of congress, a politician, is that correct?"

"That is correct, Frank, and I am in the process of running for governor."

"My…my in the process of running for governor, are we? Obviously this polygraph examination is extremely important to you. For if it takes a turn for the worst it will affect your career and perhaps your party, is that right Harry?"

"That is correct, Frank."

"And you Sydney, who are you?"

Sydney looked up at me after folding his arms and placing them on his bulging stomach in a defensive position, "I'm sorry, Mr. Legion for being sheepish with you, but as I have implied already, of which you have now become aware of, my utmost concern is that the sensitivity and secrecy of this matter is of the utmost importance and be kept strictly among us.

But to answer your question forthwith, I am Harry's personal legal attorney and his campaign manager for his run on the governorship. Understand, Mr. Legion?"

"Yes I understand, please call me, Frank." I stated.

"Thank you, Frank. As I was saying, an incident of sexual impropriety could have disastrous effects on both Harry's and my career, not mentioning the political party we adhere to. So even the slightest mention of Harry taking a polygraph examination is quite hazardous for us. Surely you can understand?"

"Of course, Sydney, I understand, the sensitivity of this matter and the damaging effect it could have on Harry. I should state that by law, polygraph material and the examination as a whole has attorney client privilege. So none of the material, can or will be released provided you two and that clandestine camera pointed at me doesn't talk."

But I should warn you that if somehow this matter goes to trial and I am compelled to take the sworn oath on the sanctity of the stand by a judge, I have to release the information. For there are times judges in pretrial and such want to know privy information based on my investigation as to what precisely transpired in order to reach a more correct verdict."

"I see…. I see," Sydney stated.

"Do you two want to start telling me the whole story and is this a felony or misdemeanor?" I asked.

Sydney stated bluntly, "We hope neither and that this case is based on false allegations. A simple he-she situation, we like to think that may have been done for extortion purposes."

"Fine, lets get on with it, shall we?" I asked.

"Can I ask two questions," Harry asked.

"Sure, go ahead." I stated.

"Frank, is it normal that people are nervous prior to taking a polygraph examination?"

"Yes, just about everyone taking a polygraph examination is nervous, Harry. It is tantamount to having a colonoscopy, it is something you have to do but your ill at ease doing it." I stated.

Sydney chuckling, "That's one way of putting it."

"People being nervous for a polygraph examination is normal yet it tells me one of two things. First the person is truthful and they see their life passing before them because of their fear of being incorrectly diagnosed.

While on the other hand, a deceptive person is also concerned because he is aware that he is going up against *something* that he truly don't understand and that *something* will expose his deceit." I stated.

"This is my career and I am very nervous about this," Harry stated.

"I understand," I replied, "assume the worst and pray for the best Harry that the alleged victim doesn't file against you."

"Huh…huh," Harry stated, "my second question is, does Sydney have to leave the room when we develop the questions?"

"No, as long as you two corroborate the questions, I don't have a problem with that." I stated. "But understand, you have to pass all the questions I ask you to pass and not just a majority."

"I understand...okay," Harry, stated. "I am giving Sydney veto power over the questions."

"Fine," I replied, "Let me ask you this, does this incident have anything to do with the military, and if so, will I be dealing with JAG officers?"

"No," Harry stated.

"Okay, tell me the story," I asked. "As I understand from the briefs here, you are being accused of sexually harassing a female employee, correct?"

Sydney jumped in, "Yes, that is correct, per Harry's and my understanding after review with his attorney, Mr. Cabman. There are certain questions we need asked and would prefer only these questions be asked."

"Okay," I stated, "as long as it covers the issue and is not detrimental to my investigation. The bottom line is you have to be asked all the elements of this alleged crime in order to be cleared of it.

However if you feel your own questions designed by council will suffice to clear you, that'll work."

Sydney replied, "Yes, we believe these questions will suffice, Frank, and they are written here on this sheet of paper."

Sydney handed me the piece of paper.

"Hmm...," As I looked at the piece of paper.

Sydney then stated, "The story goes like this, Frank, last May, Harry and Kim were working here alone after hours of preparation for his campaign for governor.

Kim had a bottle of wine, which she purchased earlier that day during lunch break and according to her story she was going to take it home after work. As the work continued late into the evening, she asked Harry if she could open the bottle and pour herself a drink. Harry stated he didn't mind so Kim poured herself a drink and being polite, poured Harry one also.

As Harry and Kim continued to work up until midnight, they finished the bottle together.

They then decided to call it a day and began closing up shop, when according to Kim, Harry approached her and pinned her to the wall and demanded sex. She alleges, she stated no and just pushed him away figuring the wine had affected Harry. Not wanting to create a scene with her boss she attempted to get away.

At this time she further alleged Harry grabbed her and pinned her against the wall again and forcefully kissed her. Kim then stated while Harry pinned her to the wall he grabbed both her breasts and then her inner thigh. She screamed, pushed him away and then ran out of the office stating she was going to press charges against him."

I looked at Harry and asked, "Harry, what Sydney just told me, is any of this true?"

"No, I don't remember any of this, I think she set me up for a fall," Harry replied.

"Well, Harry, why would Kim make up a story like this?" I asked.

Harry responded, "I'm ashamed to say it, but Kim thought she had a better grasp of my campaign strategy then Sydney or I did. So I told her earlier in the day, perhaps too bluntly to stick to her secretary duties. I think she was pretty sore over it.

I do admit to bumping into her inadvertently as we were closing up."

"Let me ask you these questions Harry and just answer with a yes or no, okay?

"All right," Harry replied.

So I questioned him as follows:

(1) Did you ever attempt to kiss your secretary Kim without her permission? (NO)

(2) Did you ever sexually harass your secretary Kim at any time? (NO)

(3) Did you ever touch or caress Kim's thigh for sexual gratification? (NO)

(4) Did you ever grab both breasts of your secretary, Kim, at anytime? (NO)

(5) Did you ever forcefully pin your secretary Kim against the wall and ask her for sex? (NO)

I then finished with, "Harry are you ready for testing?"

"Yes, I am," Harry, responded.

"I have a question for you Harry, in your life have you ever been falsely accused of something you did not do?"

Harry looking up and to the left stated, "Ahh…. yes a motorcycle ticket for speeding about five years ago. Lying to members of congress over certain bills."

"Is that all, nothing more?" I asked.

"Nothing more…that's all," Harry answered.

As we began the examination I asked Harry all the questions we had just reviewed. I could see Harry was developing a mysterious cough while his heartbeat sitting down was 102 beats per minute and increasing. His blood pressure parameter was climbing exponentially as if they were mountains. His breathing revealed deceptive stair casing patterns across the charts on the relevant questions.

I said to myself, hoping to pass my first politician in my career today but my hopes were cut short as Harry's chart showed consistent deception.

Looking at Harry's troubled eyes I had to break him the bad news, which was tantamount to some telling people that they have terminal cancer.

As Sydney walked back into the room both he and Harry looked at me with their thousand-yard stare as they awaited my results.

"Well, Harry, there's no way of saying this except to say it straight out. You were inconclusive failing and if I continued testing you, you would have failed outright. I stopped the examination the moment when I knew you couldn't pass. This was done to give you an inconclusive failing on your report but not a total failure. That said, it is my strong recommendation that you do not take a polygraph examination with a public examiner. "

Harry looking at the floor with a grim look on his face said nothing.

Sydney realizing the gravity of the situation stated, "Obviously this is distressing for we had hoped for a more positive response."

"I too had hoped for a more positive response, Sydney, but if I passed Harry I would be lying to him. Furthermore, I would be misleading him into failure if he had to take an examination before a public examiner. Simply said Sydney, they would hang him if he gave them the same polygraph charts he gave me."

Sydney regaining his professional demeanor stated, "Thank you, Mr. Legion, for your time and professional opinion on this matter. Again, we trust this matter will go no farther then these four walls.

Lastly, we don't feel the need for a written report for your verbal answer has sufficed."

As I was escorted out of the office at double time, I glanced back at Harry who had the look of a man whose world had just came crashing down.

According to the upcoming stories that were published on the front pages of state distributed daily newspapers, he was right.

## Chapter 9 - "Brothers and sisters, do I get an amen?"

After having a small lunch I drove down Interstate 65 to a city named Southport, Indiana, not far from the capitol.

Using the map given to me by Mr. Cabman's secretary, I located the address in question of the person who wanted to remain anonymous.

I said to myself this cloak and dagger stuff sometimes gets the best of me for it was like being a gladiator in the coliseum of life awaiting the verdict from Emperor Nero. In this game it is better to quit on top then face the lions from Nero.

At times it is only the money that keeps me going for I am the type of person who does not like to emerge into or know of another person's dirty laundry.

Whoever this guy may be, he allegedly paid his attorney $1,000 dollars for me to administer one examination that takes on average two to three hours to complete.

As I approached the security gate for the condominium complex, I told the security guard that a gentleman was expecting me at 333 Stony Croft Lane and could he direct me.

The security guard politely gave me the directions and stated that a Mr. Jalen Putinbay resided there and was expecting me.

Arriving at the condominium, I knocked on the door and was met by a well-dressed middle-aged black male.

He introduced himself as, Mr. Jalen Putinbay, and invited me into the living room where he formally introduced me to his black lady companion, whom he identified only as Jasmin.

As I set up my equipment and showed them both my license, I told them I was here on behalf of their attorney and would like to know what this matter was about.

He stated his problem was simple and he only wanted one question asked and one question only.

I then stated, "Mr. Putinbay, you're entitled to five or six questions regarding your problem, are you sure you don't want more?"

"No, one question will do Mr. Legion. By the way can I call you Frank and please call me, Jalen."

"Yes, Frank's fine."

"Frank, I called you here because it was the only way Jasmin would take the polygraph examination."

"That's fine I've been making house and office calls for 32 years, Jalen. Now what can I do for you?"

"Well, to the point Frank, Jasmin and I are planning on getting married soon, but there is a certain concern of mine that I heard through the grapevine that Jasmin may be sexually cheating on me.

We have been going together for 8 years and I want to clear the slate if she has been faithful to me or not."

"Okay," as I looked over at Jasmin. "Is there any truth to the allegation, Jasmin?"

"No, none whatsoever," Jasmin stated.

As I looked at Jasmin, I could readily see that she was eloquent, gracious and very beautiful. Besides that, she was well dressed, intelligent and focused.

It is known in certain circles among polygraph examiners that the most honest and purest polygraph charts can be obtained from southern black females, who are Baptists. I don't know precisely why, but I suspect honesty was deeply engrained in them from birth. Moreover, they are sincerely a God fearing people which led me to wonder if Jasmin could be one of these rare birds that I have witnessed from time to time throughout my career.

It was kind of like being a bird enthusiast who comes from all over the world to Mid-Michigan in hopes of spotting a very rare finch known as a Kirkland Warbler.

During my tenure in the polygraph business, I considered this type of person to be among the most purest and honest of the human species, they are truly unique.

"So if I understand you right, Jalen, the question you and Jasmin want me to ask would be, "Since you have been going with Jalen, have you had sex with any other person? Is that correct?"

Both answered, "Yes."

I then started my pretest interview and true to form, Jasmin answered everything exactly as I predicted. She was a schoolteacher who sang in her church choir and was sweet and articulate. White women didn't have anything over her for she was a real stand-alone beauty. Not only on the outside was Jasmin beautiful but also within where beauty really counts.

Though as stated by law, I could not ask her, her religion. Yet I was curious. But as luck would have it, she inadvertently stated she was Baptist, which made my day.

So as I continued through this "cake walk" examination, Jasmin answered all my "hidden meaning questions" precisely as a truthful person would answer. Her story line, demeanor and body language was spot on. She was picture perfect and I was highly certain she would pass with flying colors.

As we went through the battery of tests I could see that each of her charts were perfect, a real gem to behold, a Mona Lisa.

I had another Kirtland Warbler and it made my day.

At times like this, I say to myself why would a man pay $1,000 dollars to have his lover take a polygraph examination when it was obvious she was as pure as the driven snow.

At this time, I advised Jasmin she had passed her examination with flying colors, yet she didn't look surprise at all for apparently she expected it.

Yet Jalen did look surprised.

Why is that I wondered?

Jalen then approached me and stated, "Frank, what do you think of this women?"

"Well, Jalen, off the record what I see is a very beautiful person on the outside and inside. I further see a gracious lady who is intelligent, honest and soft-spoken. She looks like a wonderful woman to me."

Jalen then stated, "If you were me, Frank, would you marry her?"

I looked at Jasmin and stated to Jalen, "Absolutely, for I hate to see good things go to waste. Moreover, Jasmin is one of the few types of woman, I would take home to my mother."

"Thank you, Mr. Legion, I'll escort you to your car."

At that time, Jalen paid me $1,000 dollars in cash, which caught me by surprise, for usually the attorney's firm pays the bill.

As I was walking to my vehicle, Jalen then stopped me and stated, "Mr. Legion, could I ask you to run another examination?"

"On Jasmin?" I asked.

"No, another friend, who lives about 3 miles down the road."

"Same matter," as he seriously looked at me.

I said to myself, the plot thickens, what the hell is this all about? I knew there was something seedy about this guy. Plus he's formally addressing me now, why the change?

"Okay, 3 miles down the road, you say?" I asked.

"Yes, Mr. Legion, just follow me. But I do not want you to tell the person you're about to examine that you tested Jasmin or mention anything about this case. In other words, just come in cold as if this next person is your first test?"

"Okay," I stated.

Jalen then handed me another $1,000 dollars in cash.

As we drove to a very beautiful house on Woodmere Street, in Southport, I watched him enter the home. I decided to wait another 10 minutes and let things settle down while I checked my gun and turned my taped recorder on.

After leaving a voice mail on my whereabouts at the home office and Tracy and Kelly's cell phone, I approached the home cautiously and then knocked on the door.

Jalen greeted me again and introduced himself as Mr. Putinbay, as if we never met.

He then walked me through his beautiful multi-level home and introduced me to a beautiful middle age black lady named, Aaliyah.

We gracefully acknowledge each other and I began my polygraph spill all over again. I couldn't help but wonder what Jalen was trying to do, but my answer came when Aaliyah further identified herself as Jalens's wife of 14 years.

I said to myself, damn it, Jasmin was a mistress but why would he want to test his wife, if he is cheating?

As our conversation warmed up, I could see not only was Aaliyah beautiful on the outside but on the inside she was more beautiful then Jasmin. Hard to believe back to back, but Aaliyah beat Jasmin in all aspects, hands down. Jalen`s wife, Aaliyah, was better all around then his mistress, Jasmin. What was Jalen up to, I thought?

Now, Jalen focused the conversion by stating that he wanted his lovely wife to take a polygraph examination regarding her fidelity during 14 years of marriage.

Inside I was angry, but I covered my feelings and asked Aaliyah if she wanted to take a polygraph examination.

She stated yes because she loved her husband and was doing this on his behalf.

I looked down at the wooden floor and then looked at Jalen with contempt.

"What questions do you want me ask you, Aaliyah?"

Jalen jumped in and stated, "We only want one question asked and only one?"

Hearing this before, I stated, "Let me guess, since you Aaliyah, have been married to Jalen have you had sex with any other person?"

"That's correct." Jalen stated.

So I started the polygraph examination, realizing that I may have two back-to-back Kirtland Warbler's for the first time in my career. As the pretest continued, Aaliyah answered every question perfectly as if she was reading from a script. Though I knew she wasn't briefed she definitely stood a cut above most woman, like my late wife was, who when placed on this earth gave their body, mind and spirit to their husband and children.

She told me she was a church going woman, a Baptist, and thanked God every day for Jalen and their children.

Needless to say, I was deeply troubled by what Jalen was doing but I continued with my examination in the hopes of exonerating Aaliyah.

As I completed the examination the results were predictable, I informed Aaliyah that she had passed her examination with flying colors and her charts were among the most perfect charts I have ever seen in nearly 32 years.

Jalen gently kissed his wife on the lips stating how much he loved her. Though Jalen was black, the look in his eyes for a microsecond showed me his soul was blacker.

Yet as Jalen pulled away from the kiss, Aaliyah's facial expression told me she was a woman who knew she was being betrayed.

I asked her if the results surprised her?

She then stated she knew she would pass and wasn't surprised at all.

As a matter of fact, neither was I except for having two perfect examinations back to back. This was a first in the polygraph industry as far as I knew.

Though Jalen continued to play the roll, he was surprised about the outcome and had a confused look on his face.

I said to myself what the hell does that mean, why isn't he jubilant?

They both thanked me and in a sudden rush Jalen led me to the front door out of earshot of Aaliyah, where I told him he has a very wonderful wife and may want to reconsider what he was doing.

He said nothing.

So as I was leaving out the front door I had to ask Jalen what he did for a living?

"Mr. Putinbay, do you mind if I ask you what do you do for a living?"

"No, I don't mind, Mr. Legion. I am an ordained Minister, preaching in the name of the Lord, Halleluiah."

I was stunned; he was playing one woman for marriage and the other he was betraying.

He then stated without any concern or remorse, "Would you like to join my church and congregation?"

I felt like I was going to puke and lost it figuring the $2,000 dollars I made for the work that I did most probably came from the congregation's hat money.

So in the spur of the moment in which has only happened a few times in my career, I told my client what I thought.

"Jalen, your preaching from the pulpit to the sheep of Jesus Christ and adultery means nothing to you?

Jesus's flock has been scattered for over two thousand years and a remnant of them have come to you for help and you are deliberately misleading them.

Your congregation comes to you for leadership and direction, as Jesus has commanded you to feed his sheep. Yet you violate your marriage vows and oath of office without concern while wearing the cloth of a preacher.

You have become a wolf in sheep's clothing.

This money you gave me is it yours or your parishioners? You play sugar daddy to your mistress while cheating on your wife, while preaching in the name of the Lord.

Do as I say but not as I do…. is that how this works?

And in your final act you lead two beautiful and wonderful women astray.

One of which is your wife, Reverend.

For a wife is not something to keep until you find something better, but to keep until death do us part?

Correct me if I'm wrong?

Is not that what our master said?

Even though this money is not mine to give, I wish I could give back your blood money but we run a business here and I know you would just use it for your own selfish enterprise.

How deep must hell be to hide you from your shame?"

Jalen closed the door in my face.

My, my, I mumbled, *"You betray your master and wife with a kiss?"*

I stood there for a moment, pissed off, with the steal door two inches from my face. But after cooling off I walked back to my car shaking my head, thinking what Jesus said two thousand years ago, *"When I return, will I find faith on the earth?"*

I don't know Lord, I don't know.

## Chapter 10 - *"Wolves in sheep's clothing"*

The next day I got back to Mr. Cabman's office and prior to leaving for court he introduced me to his client, Dominique Z. Tucker II.

As we sat down together, I was informed that Mr. Tucker was accused of raping three young girls who were all under the age of thirteen. The case facts revealed that he lured them in at different times and that they were all members of his family.

When we completed all the legal paperwork, I stated to the examinee, "Mr. Tucker are you aware of the duration of prison time you could do for these alleged acts of Criminal Sexual Conduct and Accosting For Immoral Purposes?

Based on the complaint, you have eight felony counts against you of which four are life sentences plus 60 years as a chaser."

"That's a long time, but I swear I didn't do it." He said.

"The complaint states Mr. Tucker, that the first child, your granddaughter, Bobbi Jo, you had sexual intercourse with her. Furthermore, you committed cunnilingus on her multiple times on different dates. It also states you forced her to commit the sexual act of fellatio on you. Is that true?"

"No…no…it's not true?"

"Mr. Tucker the complaint also states that you stuck your penis or finger in her rectum. Is that true?"

Mr. Tucker looking down at the floor and tightly rubbing his hands together stated softly, "No, that's a lie also."

"The complaint continues by stating that the second child also a granddaughter of yours, Cyndi-Bet, has accused you of having sexual intercourse with her on multiple occasions and fingering her anus while both of you were in your pickup truck. Is that true?"

I could see Mr. Tucker was breaking a sweat and probably was predisposed that by paying his attorney for the polygraph examination insured he would pass. From the get-go it didn't look good for the home team.

"Cyndi-Bet made that up, no way would I do that, that's a lie also."

"Did I say eight counts Mr. Tucker, I was wrong? I see here on the back page of this complaint a ninth count.

This complaint states that you, did accost, entice and solicit the services of Vicki-Lynn, by forcing and inducing your third underage granddaughter to have sexual intercourse with you.

You further lured her into the act of gross indecency, or other acts of depravity or delinquency by encouraging this child to have sex with you. Is that true?"

Mr. Tucker replied, "I admit, I have heat down below, Mr. Legion, but I wouldn't do these things to my granddaughters."

I humored him, "I'm glad to hear you didn't commit these criminal acts against three children. That makes my day and my job easier, Mr. Tucker."

"I hope to prove my innocence today, Mr. Legion and walk out of here a free man."

"Well, I don't know if your going to walk out of here today a free man, Mr. Tucker, based solely on a polygraph examination but hopefully it will help support your claim that your innocent."

"I hope so too, Mr. Legion. I feel this whole thing is a misunderstanding by family members about me."

"Why Mr. Tucker, whatever do you mean? Are you saying your family thinks that lowly of you to have you sent away for life in prison based on some idiosyncrasy?"

"I just think they all ganged up on me for the moment and wanted me out of their lives forever, Mr. Legion."

"Hell of a going away party. With friends like that who needs enemies, Mr. Tucker?"

With a staged smile, "Yah, your right, Mr. Legion, and here I thought my family were my friends. Apparently I was wrong."

"Well, Mr. Tucker, their charges claim you committed, cunnilugus, fellatio and digital penetration with their underage daughters. It further states that you had sexual intercourse with them, which sounds to me like you got your work cut out for you unless you pass my polygraph examination."

"Well, I believe at the end of the day this polygraph examination will corroborate my testimony that I am telling the truth with respect to the allegations, Mr. Legion."

"Good to hear that. By the way you can call me Frank and I'll call you Dominique unless you object?"

"No problem, Frank."

"Good then lets get into this shall we and sort out facts from fiction, Dominique.

But before we start I want to advise you that you must pass all the polygraph questions I am about to ask you and anything less then that constitutes a failure, understood?"

"Yes, loud and clear, Frank."

"I understand all these girls are your granddaughters by blood, is that correct?"

"Yes, that is correct, Frank?"

I couldn't help but notice Dominique knee's shaking violently despite the room being warm. His body language revealed he was evasive and deceptive. He definitely didn't look right, his eyes started blinking like a strobe light and he kept looking over his right shoulder "rubbernecking", as if someone was coming in to shoot him.

Hopefully, I will not be caught in the crossfire.

"Dominique, have you ever been treated by a psychiatrist?"

Dominique hesitated, then blurted out, "Yes, Frank, about sixty times. I was diagnosed as a manic depressant with suicidal thoughts all the time."

"Dominique, have you ever been arrested before?"

Dominique replied, "Yes, Criminal Sexual Conduct with a child but the case was dropped due to lack of evidence and a felonious assault charge by a female hooker who stated I hit her with a chair. Though later the case was also dropped after the hooker failed to show for trial. They found her body floating face down in Ohio's, Maumee River two days after my trial was over."

"Suicide or suicided?" I smirk.

"She was beaten with a blunt instrument, Frank."

"My...my, in case your attorney hasn't already advised you, Dominique, that if your bound over to circuit court the judge shall order you to be tested for venereal disease.

Furthermore, you will be tested for hepatitis B infection and for the presence of HIV or HIV antibodies.

Then if your convicted of these felonies a court order shall be given forthwith to collect DNA identification profiling samples from you.

Hopefully, this will not lead to you being connected to other crimes besides this nine-count complaint.

`So it is important you level with me right now, Dominique, otherwise your placing yourself in harms way. For if you play games with me today and the prosecutors public polygraph examiner, well as the saying goes, "Your done like dinner."

As I looked at Dominique and pondered past experiences that I learned over the years in the streets of cities certain observations came to mind. That it is highly suspicious when a person is always malingering around the crime scenes that there is a fair to high probability that he is a player in those crimes.

For I have witnessed many a time criminals returning to the crime scene and stand in the crowd of onlookers playing like their curiosity got the best of them.

But when I arrived at the scene I just wouldn't look at the victim, oh no, but rather eyeball the crowd and try to get a mental image of the gawkers.

There was even times when I would have the evidence technicians at the crime scene pretend they taking pictures of the victim, but in fact they were taking pictures of the crowd.

More often then not the perpetrator was in that crowd and it was a good starting point if the case didn't have any leads.

"Dominique, have you ever been falsely accused of something you did not do?"

"Nothing."

As I raised my eyebrows, "Nothing at all Dominique?"

"Nothing."

"What do you think Dominique should happen to a person if they did these terrible things?"

"I think Frank, they should give him another chance or be given counseling."

"So, then Dominique, you don't feel they should get prison time in anyway?"

"No, I think Frank another chance would be the most appropriate means of administering justice."

"Okay," I stated, "tell me what you remember Dominique, lets hear the story?"

"Well, Frank, after my sons found out that their daughters were complaining about me sexually molesting them, they decided to have a talk with me.

We discussed the matter and decided in order to stay friends they would take me to a psychiatrist for counseling and therapy.

I agreed and while being treated by the psychiatrist, I mentioned to him that I love punishment and pain."

"Hmmm…okay, continue Dominique."

"I admitted to my sons that I did touch their daughters private areas."

"When you say you touched their private areas Dominique, do you mean their vagina?"

"Ahh…yes. Dominique stated.

"How old were they when you allegedly touched their vagina and other private area, Dominique?"

"Ahh…. approximately five to seven years old."

When they were five to seven years old did you touch their buttocks, Dominique?"

"I probably did, but I am not sure."

"Did you touch their inner thigh and breasts, when they were five to seven years old?"

"Yes and it was because of this that I decided to go to counseling so my sons and I could stay friends."

"Dominique, are there any other allegations about you molesting children not in this court complaint?"

"Yes, another neighborhood girl named Deborah claims I had fondled her private areas also and had sex with her."

"Did you." I asked.

"Not that I recall Frank."

"Hmmm…. are you saying you have another case pending besides this case?"

146

"Yes, there are two more cases that are pending besides this case, Frank."

"And these two cases involve you and underage children, Dominique?"

"Yes."

"What are they stating you did?"

"They are saying I did oral sex on them?"

"How old were they?" I asked.

"About seven years old." Dominique stated.

I couldn't help but say to myself that either Dominique is extremely unlucky with children or he is one sick puppy. Obviously I believed the latter.

"Have you ever committed the sexual act of cunnilingus with any of your grandchildren?"

"No."

"Have you ever had fellatio by any of your grandchildren?"

"No."

"Have you ever conducted digital penetration in the vagina or anus with any of your grandchildren?"

"No."

"Have you ever had sexual penetration in anyway with any of your granddaughters?"

"No."

"So again Dominique, you admitted to me that you did touch all your grandchildren in their private areas? Flesh to flesh."

"Yes."

"So if I understand your strategy, you admit to and agree to jail time for Criminal Sexual Conduct in the fourth degree for touching your granddaughters private areas, "flesh to flesh."

But you don't agree to Criminal Sexual Conduct in the first degree having sex with your granddaughters which will result in three life sentences, am I correct, Dominique?"

"Yes."

"So you know your going down one way or another, Dominique?"

"Yes."

"Okay, here's the deal Dominique, this whole matter gets down to whether you sexually penetrated your three grandchildren or had oral sex with them, right?"

"Right."

"Therefore, Dominique, I'm not going to go through all these hundred of pages of reports when it all gets down to penetration?"

"That's right."

"So the questions I just asked you, in which you answered no to, are the questions that you will be tested on?"

"Could you repeat them again?"

"Sure, "Have you ever had committed the sexual act of cunnilingus with any of your grandchildren?

Have you ever-committed fellatio with any of your grandchildren?

Have you ever conducted digital penetration in the vagina or anus with any of your grandchildren?

Have you ever had sexual penetration in anyway with any of your granddaughters?

You answered no to all of those questions Dominique."

"That's right," Dominique answered.

"Since we agree on these questions, I will begin testing you now Dominique?"

Throughout the next two hours, I tested Dominique through a battery of six exams to ensure a low probability of error, if any.

As I watched him squirm, he reminded me of the exam that was done on that well-known sports player, "Otay Gypsum", who took a polygraph examination in private at the behest of his high-powered attorneys.

The creeping crud failed his examination, with a numerical score of -22 for the murder of his wife and her lover. A numerical score of –6 or more was failure, therefore "Otay" failed so badly that he could have failed three more people besides himself.

At this time his attorneys destroyed the charts by flushing them down the toilet. They then claim to the public that no polygraph examination has been given to their client because they do not believe in them. All the while, "Otay" claimed he didn't know he was taking a real polygraph examination but rather a practice test.

In any case the public did not know that so the jury let him go because they didn't understand DNA, therefore they claimed because "Otay" didn't fit, they must acquit!"

I learned long ago that, "I can't cure dumb" for, "Stupid is as stupid does."

When the examination was completed Dominique failed every question, every time and I informed Mr. Cabman of such.

Dominique's freedoms as he knew it was over, for the plea-bargaining did not work and he would go on to spend the rest of his days in prison.

## Chapter 11 - *"A Book by it's Cover"*

The following day, Kelly and I arrived at "the grubs" girlfriend's home for our polygraph examination. As we walked up to the examinee's home, Kelly and I had to stop and marvel at a herd of buffalo that was grazing on the top of the hill.

Sandra, the grub's girlfriend, a tall and attractive brunette graciously welcomed us into her old colonial house that was smack in the middle of a quaint farming community.

As we sat down by the kitchen table, Sandra began to tell us her story and concern.

She began by stating, she was a divorced lady with a fifteen-year-old daughter, Shirley.

According to Sandra, she had the intentions to marry a man named, Lee, a.k.a, "the grub", who had proposed to her. Sandra then went on to say that Shirley did not like Lee because she claimed he had molested her in the past.

Sandra stated she didn't know whom to believe because Shirley was a chronic liar, yet the thought of marrying a man who may have molested her daughter terrified her to death. Shirley informed Sandra that about a month ago Lee had grabbed her by the breast and forced her to give him oral sex and have sexual intercourse with him on the living room sofa.

Kelly then asked her if a police report had been made or was social services notified. Sandra stated she did not inform either service yet. Further she did not have a doctor check Shirley for vaginal penetration.

I then asked Sandra if Shirley was at home so we could question her and where was Lee? Sandra stated Shirley was at her grandmothers about fifty miles away and refused to stay at home here until Lee vacated the premises. Sandra then told us that Lee had just texted her that he was enroute to her location and should be arriving shortly to take the polygraph examination.

Sandra stated she would greet Lee outside and stay in her pickup truck until the examination was over. A short time later Lee arrived and drove up the dirt driveway.

When Sandra went out to greet him, I could see why he was referred to as "the grub". He had to be the filthiest and dirtiest person I had ever seen take a polygraph examination. Hell, he looked worst then a grub but rather like a damn troll who had been living under a bridge for a year without washing. I mean this guy looked like he just got pulled out of a tar pit. If dress was an indicator of character he was sure to fail.

Kelly looked at me and stated, "Damn talk about a dirty old man, he is filthy. Certainly he is going to fail uncle. If he smells as bad as he looks were both going to be sick before this test is over. No wonder the attorneys didn't want him tested in their office.

"Thank God, Kelly, he is not our first test."

At this time, Lee opened the front screen door and entered in. We both introduced ourselves but were hesitant on extending our hand in friendship due to sanitary reasons. Lee stunk to high heaven as we surmised. He stunk like an outhouse in mid July. Oh, man, I said to myself, this is going to be a tough three hours as I remembered that smelly fat lady I had as a fireman. Why can't people take a shower before an exam, I mean it's only your life at stake?

We opened our playing hand by Kelly sitting at the kitchen table with Lee while I sat back on the sofa pretending I was reading a sports magazine. Kelly stated, "Mr. Lee, there are allegations that you have had illegal sex with a minor at different locations and times. Furthermore, the allegations are such that this minor said you have forced her to give you oral sex and that you had sexual intercourse with her along with vaginally penetrating her vagina with your finger against her will."

The victim is the daughter of your girlfriend, Sandra, who goes by the name Shirley and is a fifteen-year-old juvenile.

Lee responded, "I love Sandra with all my heart but Shirley doesn't like me because I don't give her money."

"Okay", Kelly responded, "What does that mean?"

Lee stated, "Well, it means because I don't give Shirley money and she wants her mother to go back to her father that she fabricated this story by saying I had sex with her."

Kelly staring at Lee, "So you're saying then that the allegations are false, is that correct?"

"Yes Ma`m", Lee stated, "That is correct. I love Sandra with all my heart and Shirley is doing everything to destroy our relationship."

Kelly came back, "Is that the reason why you believe Shirley has come up with this story."

"Yes, that is what I believe", Lee reiterated.

Kelly then asked Lee if he is complying to take a polygraph examination, "Mr. Lee are you willing to take a polygraph examination to clear yourself of these allegations that you're being accused of?"

Lee expressed his feelings, "I don't want the test, but because I love Sandra so much I'll take the examination."

I then jumped in, "You know, Mr. Lee, that if you fail your polygraph examination or if Sandra becomes suspicious you failed she may ultimately go to social services and then the police department. So you may be opening a whole can of worms for yourself. I mean having sex with a minor, that is, grabbing her breast is Criminal Sexual Conduct-Second Degree, a fifteen-year felony. Plus having sexual intercourse with an underage child is life or any term of years, mandatory minimum is twenty-five years and a lifetime of electronic monitoring. What I'm stating to you Mr. Lee is that if you believe right now that your going to compromise your well-being, I suggest you tell us you did it and don't take the test."

"Sir," Lee stated, "If I did what Shirley stated I would kill myself, because I couldn't live with myself. I want to take the test to show Sandra that I love her and that I'm telling the truth."

Kelly asked, "Lee what opinion do you have of yourself."

Lee stated, "I'm a God fearing decent man."

Kelly questioned him, "Have you ever been falsely accused of anything in you life, Lee?"

"Yes, this", Lee stated spontaneously.

"If we asked you did you ever have sex with Shirley, how would you answer that," asked Kelly.

Lee stated, "I would say, no."

Kelly then stated, "If we asked you did you ever grab Shirley's breast, how would you answer that?"

Lee again stated, "I would say no to that also."

"If we asked you did you ever have sexual intercourse with Shirley, how would you answer that Lee?"

"Again I would say no, Ms."

"If we asked you did you ever penetrate Shirley's vagina with anything, how would you answer that Lee?"

"No, just like all the other ones," said Lee.

If we asked you are you lying to us in anyway to give yourself an alibi in this case, how would you answer that?" Kelly stated.

"Again like all the rest, still no," Lee stated.

Kelly then stated, "Lee are you ready for testing?"

"Yes," said Lee.

Kelly asked, "How do you think the test will come out?"

"That I'm telling the truth, I hope." stated Lee.

I then asked Lee, "What do you think should happen to a person if he failed his test and did do this to an underage girl?"

"If I did do this, I'd kill myself," Lee stated.

After about two hours of testing and questioning Kelly and I went over the charts as Lee was still "hooked up". Much to our surprise his charts were perfect and he responded only to the control questions and not to the relevant questions. He passed with flying colors. The "grub" wasn't a rapist nor was he attempting to apply any counter measures. His charts were clean as a whistle so we unhooked him. We told him he passed his exam with flying colors and there was such a release of pent up tension within him for being falsely accused that his head slumped. He then collapsed on the floor weeping but it was not an ordinary cry of men but rather the release of his soul from his captors who have come to destroy him.

As I stood there looking at what was called "a grub" with his head weeping in his hands, my heart went out to him. I said to myself this guy had every exterior display that he was guilty. He was filthy, smelly and his clothes were grubby as that of a bum who had slept in them for a year.

I had to ask him, "How come you came dressed like you did, Lee, especially when you knew this test meant so much to you?"

Lee while still sobbing deeply stated, "Mister, I love Sandra so much I would do anything for her, anything at all. I give her all my money because I love her and I couldn't bear these lies Shirley said about me and the possibility that I would fail my examination just overwhelmed me.

I'm a truck mechanic sir and I work in the pits beneath the trucks. I work fifteen hours a day and seven days straight in a truck garage where I get no time off and little money. But what I get, I give to Sandra in an attempt to win her heart. I came right from work from the truck grease pit to take this test, I'm tired of being treated badly."

Kelly and I couldn't help but feel sorry for Lee's condition but thankful he passed his examination as he rose from the floor and stated, "You know mister, what I was going to do if I failed my examination because I couldn't bear the shame of being a child rapist?"

I was afraid to ask, but asked anyway, as Kelly looked at him from the kitchen table with tears in her eyes, "What were you going to do mister, if you failed?"

At this time, from his crotch area, Lee pulled out a stainless steel, Smith and Wesson .357 magnum, model 66 and put it to his head crying as if he wanted to end it.

Now Kelly about five feet from him is frozen in time and space and going into shock. I realize, damn it, that my .38 caliber police snub-nosed, Smith and Wesson, model 60 is in my briefcase five feet from me. I can't get to it. I can't get to it! I can't get to my gun without perhaps pushing Lee into a nuclear meltdown. As I attempt to talk to him in the hopes of calming him down, Lee then pulls the hammer back on the revolver while it is still pushed against his left temple.

Kelly is petrified.

I stated, "Lee you passed your examination, you don't want to hurt yourself, please put the gun down. You want to be with Sandra now and Shirley was lying, put the gun down!"

What seemed like forever, but perhaps only fifteen seconds, Lee uncocked the hammer and pulled his .357 magnum from his head.

Breathing now, I tried to comfort Lee by sympathizing with him as I slowly drifted towards my briefcase that was holding my .38 caliber revolver.

Kelly isn't moving, but at least her eyes are blinking now.

Then Lee sat down as if nothing had happened and looked at the tabletop and stated, "Thank you for passing me."

I stated, "You told the truth Lee and passed yourself."

Sandra came in and I told her Lee had passed his test. Sandra cried and put her arms around him and kissed him. She thanked us. I advised Sandra that Lee had a gun but she didn't seem concerned at all, as a matter of fact, she looked as if she understood the situation.

Kelly came out of her hibernation and slowly started putting away our equipment. I stayed by my briefcase until Kelly had all our equipment secured. As we left the house and sat in our car, Kelly couldn't shake that one thousand yard stare.

I had to say to Kelly, "We go in God's hands Kelly, apparently it wasn't our time. Kelly what I told you and Tracy earlier you now know. Our fate and destiny are held on such slender threads.

If you don't mind me telling you Kelly about a simple event that happened to me a couple months ago. I was dispatched to Detroit in the inner city for some elderly black woman, "a cougar", who had married some younger black guy.

Well she was upset because every time she would wash his work pants, she would find blonde hairs in the zipper area. So she suspected her young buck was walking the Cass Corridor and spending money and time with the prostitutes. So she called me to test her husband who agreed to take the test but was very reluctant.

In cases like these Kelly, especially in inner city Detroit, you always go armed and inform dispatch or Coco when you arrive at location and when you leave location.

Further, you call in just after the pretest interview and before you place the attachments on the subject. When you call in, use encrypted color code, green, yellow, and red as to your safety status. Code green if everything is okay. Code yellow if things are going bad and that you will prematurely be exiting the scene. While code red is like in police work, that is, you're in imminent danger or fear of your life and you need backup.

If dispatch hears code red she notifies all of us armed polygraph examiners and investigators with police background to respond immediately to said location.

On this particular day, when I walked in this Detroit home little did I know this big black buck had a semi-automatic pistol in his trousers just like this examinee had today.

Everything looked code green up till I went to place the attachments on the buck, when I inadvertently dropped the Galvanic Skin Response electrode on the floor. When I bent over to pick it up from below the table where the buck was sitting at I could see the buck had his semi automatic pistol pointed directly at my groin. Immediately, I knew this guy was about to be caught in a lie and he was going out in glory. So I nonchalantly responded back to my briefcase and pulled out my snub nose .38 caliber and kept it hidden from his view from behind the briefcase but it was pointed directly at his head.

He looked at me and stated, "What's wrong?"

When I told him, "You remember that police badge that I showed you prior to starting the examination that I laid on the kitchen table? You failed to think it through, friend. For it's not just a badge to impress you, but rather it means I'm a cop and that I holding a gun with a notch on it and it is pointed directly at your friggen head!

Now, you people called me for an examination, I didn't call you. So if you don't want the examination then don't waste my time, it's called common courtesy. Now put your gun on the table. I'm not moving one iota until I see your hands on the table and the gun. To my surprise the idiot started laughing and put the gun on the table.

"Why did you do that?" I responded, as I put my gun down and began closing shop to depart this volatile area.

When the idiot said, "Because, I knew I was going to fail my examination for friggen all those blonde whores on the Cass Corridor."

So I yelled back, "So you got to pull a gun on me?"

When the black cougar heard what he said about friggen all those blonde whores on the strip, she walked behind me and goes into her purse that was lying on the kitchen table. She then pulls out a semi-automatic pistol and points it at him from behind me. He responds and picks up his pistol and points it at her as I stand between them both. She begins screaming and threatening to shoot "his low down black ass" as I'm standing in the middle.

Now their both pointing their guns at each other and using me for cover while their screaming and blaming each other for the situation their in. I know, if I go for my gun the cougar will shoot me in the back for "messing with her loven man" and the buck, "with his felony warrants outstanding," will shoot me in the chest for being a white man in a black house.

You know, Kelly, you would think I would be scared shitless about this time but for some damn reason a stupid thought came to my mind in a microburst and that was how would this all look on the front page newspaper tomorrow morning?

I'm sure these idiots would have stated I was breaking and entering into their crib and they shot my lily-white ass in self-defense. Or better yet they would have dumped my ass in their neighbors dumpster then sat down to watch the television with their Malt liqueur 35 and a large bag of barbecue chips."

"There you have it, just another murder in crack town, Detroit."

"What happened then Frank?" as Kelly came out of her state of shock.

"Well Kelly, as luck would have it, the big buck cry's out, "I'm outta here" and makes a dash for the door because apparently he was more afraid of the cougar then the cop.

Not wanting to be the victim of this black rage, I make a dash for the door myself because I was more afraid of the cougar then the fleeing felon who just ran out the door in front of me.

Imagine, all this entertainment for five hundred bucks.

You know Kelly, some days I go back to the office where I just have to walk out on Luna Pier with a six pack of beer, a cigar and just stare into space."

"Frank, I didn't think this job would be that dangerous."

"Well, Kelly, I've been running examinations for over thirty years now and as far as I know, I'm the only one, *in the country*, who has been running examinations in homes that long and alone.

I cannot begin to tell you how many times I could have been killed or could have killed someone. Kelly this is how I earn my bread and butter and how I contribute in my own little way to help society.

So Kelly think seriously about the nursing field and healing people's broken bodies as compared to the polygraph field in healing people's broken souls who are falsely accused."

"I will Frank, thank you."

"Your welcome Kelly."

## Chapter 12 -"A penny for your thoughts"


As Kelly and Tracy headed back to the Luna Pier office with the polygraph reports, I instructed them that Coco was awaiting their immediate return. I advised them not to stop off at their favorite drinking and socializing hole, "Cocoa Bongo", near our Maumee Bay, Ohio office until they handed the private polygraph reports to Coco.

As for me I couldn't leave just yet for one of our seasoned investigators, Leila, who was a half hour drive away from our testing location was in a pinch and came to get me to assist in her present case.

As Leila drove me back to her testing location, which was an armor car company, I sat in the car while Leila went inside to get clearances for both of us from security.

While I sat there I couldn't help but marvel why they call these trucks armored cars. I mean it's a joke calling them armored for it appears that a .22 caliber short, if not a pellet gun could penetrate most of their outer skin.

These armored cars were always dirty, junky, and smelled as if wino's urinated in the corner of the trucks. Moreover, they were always breaking down and always in need of maintenance.

Based on my experience most of the crimes committed in this industry were of an internal nature. Much of this was based on their employees, who for the greater part were uneducated and came from the lower strata of society with all its criminal mentality.

All the time I would hear about cases where money bags were dropped off at predetermined locations along the roadway where accomplices were waiting to pickup the dough.

But the saddest case of all to me was when an armored car crew was picking up money from a bank after closing time. The black employee who was sitting shotgun in the armored car opened his door and walked around to the drivers side where this white driver, a family man of four was sitting. The black employee put two rounds in the white drivers head and killed him instantly without remorse or regret. Rufus then takes the money and gives it to his homies to hide and then calls the police claiming the armored car was robbed.

It may have worked except for the witness.

Damn, I love assisting in sending dirt bags like this to prison for the rest of their days. I almost got a full-fledged erection out of it when I saw this scumbag being dragged away in cuffs while his mama cried, "He's a good boy."

As I got called into the Security Headquarters for Bubbas Armored Car Company, I could see Leila approaching me afar. I couldn't help but marvel over her investigative skills in past cases. She was a seasoned investigator, a real digger, and a hound dog. She use to work Detroit vice for a couple years and was nicknamed "Hoover" after the vacuum cleaner because she would just arrest everybody for any reason including her mother and let GOD sort them out at the station.

After two of her police partners died unexpectedly she thought she was jinxed and gave up police work to become a private investigator and polygraph examiner.

"Leila what kind of case do you have that is causing such concern."

"Well Frank, I got this case from corporate security here at Bubbas Armored Car Company-West Branch of which I have been investigating for a couple weeks now. It is alleged that someone came into the armor car company and stole $250,000 dollars of pennies. The total weight was approximately 6,000 pounds or 3 tons that was placed within a secure garage area where it suddenly went missing over the weekend.

There are at least 15 to possibly 100 individuals that I would consider suspects in this case who could be involved in the heist of the 250,000 dollars in pennies."

"Okay, what's the problem, Leila?"

"Well, the suspects range from the armor car personnel right up to top management.

But management wants me to only polygraph one newly hired armored car driver which leads me to believe that I'm doing a partial investigation and being given the runaround."

"You probably are."

"Well, Frank, this newly hired young black guy about 22 years old, is mentally challenged though he appears honest during my initial interview. He has been with this firm for about six months now. I informed security that a thorough investigation must encompass all potential suspects who could have been involved in the theft. However, they stated management did not think it was necessary.

The money came from Coins International near Terre Haute, Indiana, where the driver, Lemont, who is the examinee, dropped off the money at Bubbas Armored Car Company West-Branch office four months ago and then gave the cage master, JoJo, the receipt.

It gets better Frank, all $250,000 of the money was sitting on pallets in a secure caged area for four months and nobody pays it any mind. That is, 125 money bags at 50 or so pounds each, weighing in over 3 tons in pennies."

"Damn…okay, Leila, I'm still following you."

"Then Frank after four months, all these pennies over a weekend just disappears…and nobody knows anything."

"Was this money Leila monitored from surveillance cameras?"

"Initially it was, but at he time of the heist or thereabout the cameras go offline just before the pennies were stolen."

"Were their any guards watching or guarding this money, Leila?"

"No, Frank, after the money was placed on the floor the guards were pulled and the alarm door sensors went out of service.

Now get this! JoJo, the cage master denies he ever received the receipt of the monies from Lemont.

Then JoJo and Lemont take a vacation during the same time frame when the heist occurs and the cameras go offline. The bags disappear into thin air in plain view of everybody but yet no one sees them go missing."

"Damn, that's one hell of a web of deceit and a big chunk of change…. literally. Did the money ever arrive at any banks?"

"No, so the F.B.I. who were involved initially in this case stated it was an internal problem and most probably someone embezzled the money from within the armored car company so they dropped the case."

"Incredible, Leila. I think we're being set up to show that an investigation was conducted so Bubba Armored Car Headquarters can get reimbursed from their insurance company while one of their fat cat manager(s) is laughing all the way to his offshore bank."

"Frank, Coins International, has the receipt that the money was taken from their location and stated it would be suffice if the armor car company polygraphed all the suspicious individuals and then be reimbursed from the armor car company's insurance policy. Bubbas Armored Car Company is trying, or appearing to try, to avoid bad press by stating they would commence their own internal investigation which came up with this twenty-two year old black armor car driver as a suspect."

"Are you telling me, Leila, that the powers that be, think this poor black guy whose probably busting his ass to feed his family lifted all of those pennies worth 250,000 dollars in plain view and that's the end of story?"

"Right, if you can believe that? The company officials stated that's all the investigation they are willing to pay us for is one polygraph examination. They told me they thought it was too costly to have all fifteen possible suspects tested."

"So, if I understand you right Leila, your concern is that the real suspects negated themselves from the investigation and handed you a patsy, a lone conspirator, who is totally clueless on the matter. In other words they are praying for a minute chance that you will fail this young black kid. Moreover, the corporate bosses must think that we are dumb enough to buy into their scam by misleading us into believing that this black guy must have had an awesome pair of booster pants to just walk off the site with 3 tons of pennies in his pants. All this, so the corporate bosses can submit the report for insurance reimbursement, is that right?"

"Yes, that appears right Frank and whoever stole the money goes scot-free. For the feds are off the case and Coins International want their money back from the insurance company and the armor car company only kicks out a thousand dollars in investigative fees."

"How deep is the rabbit hole Leila? It's almost enough to call the insurance company and tell their security bureau that we suspect this armor car company to be running a scam and that a complete investigation must be warranted before any of the $250,000 dollars in monies is paid out.

I mean this had to be premeditated and someone in the chain of command stole the money knowing that there is no one to investigate them. You and I both know that someone(s) out there is laughing his or her ass off on this heist. Yet they must be rubber necking and worried to see if anyone is on their trail.

Well, I'm going to go with you to the site and see what I can find, but remember, Leila, we run polygraph examinations and private investigations and we were not called in to investigate this by a concerned and neutral agency because it appears they don't want to know the truth. Seeing that corporate headquarters does not want the truth then just take their money, Leila.

Lets run the test on this black fellow and if he passes we'll state our concern again to corporate headquarters. Make sure your wired on this one so we can analyze the tapes later.

For this heist definitely appears to be an inside job, premeditated and a conspiracy by the bosses and the black man is being shanghaied and railroaded.

I don't know how many tests you've done with the armor car companies, Leila, but I have run numerous cases. I have found throughout the years that their work at best is substandard and their employees are paid pitifully. You would think the armor car companies who are moving all this critical bank money to and fro would have a more professional procedure in place. Despite all their highflying company names, I am yet to be impressed with any of them for they all lack accountability and professionalism.

What I'm saying Leila is that armor car companies across the board, in my opinion, do not know their right hand from their left.

Then again, when I look at your case and the safeguards that should have been in place to protect this suspicious missing money, I can only wonder if it is all being done under the guise of organized crime."

"Frank, I agree with you but what would happen if the black man fails his exam?"

"Leila, my prime directive has always been to *free the captive innocent*", if this black guy fails, I take over the case and the report. Your off the case and mums the word…you understand?"

"Yes."

"Leila, polygraph examiners pursue the truth and do not get played by some corporate stumblebums, politicians or attorneys, as a matter of fact. Some of these people think we are for sale for money and will sell our souls to the devil as they did.

*Nothing could be farther from the truth…let justice be served or let the heavens fall!"*

If Lemont fails, I'll discuss the matter with Ed when he returns and I'm fairly certain he will agree with my opinion."

"I agree Frank that we are being pulled into the middle and given the worm while the powers that be get the big fish."

"That's correct, Leila, the way I would word the report if Lemont fails, is that the examinee failed, but that the investigation was totally incomplete, bias and discriminatory in nature. In that way the insurance company will see that they have been set up and may force Bubbas Armored Car to conduct a thorough investigation before they get their monies.

Furthermore, in no way would we be implying in the report that the failure of this black patsy infers that he was acting alone in this heist or has any of the money.

That said, it is our belief that if all suspects cannot be interrogated and examined then this investigation is a "miscarriage of justice."

"And if he passes Frank?"

"Then Leila, the wolfs in sheep clothing in corporate headquarters are still at large but at least this black guy goes free.

Can we run the examination today?"

"Security stated the bosses want it tomorrow when their here."

"Okay, Leila let me review your case facts then tomorrow we'll interview the black guy together."

"Sounds like a plan, Frank."

The next day Leila and I headed over to the armor car company to examine the black armored car driver and hear his story. At the scene the usual clientele for the armored car company met us in internal security. We introduced ourselves and commenced the investigation. As always internal security was cordial and cooperative but it became readily apparent that their hands were tied by the powers over them.

Cases like this always get me madder then hell because corporate headquarters will throw blood money at our feet, in the hopes that we will turn a suspicious eye to get "the dogs" off their trail.

So our situation was this, we take the money from those who have weaved their web of deceit and in the end we leave them the fools.

Moreover, I suspect this matter will end up in a heated discussion with the top brass after they the hunters realized their being hunted.

"Mr. Frank Legion, I'm John Guppy, I'm head of security from corporate headquarters."

"Pleasure to meet you sir and this is my associate Leila, who will be handling the case today while I sit and review the particulars."

"Fine, nice meeting you, Leila."

"The pleasures mine John."

As John led us into Bubbas Armored Car conference room, we laid out our equipment and started the interview.

"John, where is the examinee?" Leila asked.

"Leila, he should be here shortly."

I then asked John to go over the facts again with both of us, for news and facts change from moment to moment during an investigation. Moreover, getting the latest information on a case was like when I was a paperboy selling the Detroit Free Press on the streets of Detroit. You "gotta" get the 5 star edition baby; otherwise you missed the latest line on the horses.

John then reiterated the facts, "Well, Frank and Leila, we know that $250,000 dollars in pennies was picked up from Coins International on December 1st, last year.

Lemont the driver took the money and gave Coins International a receipt for it and drove the money here to Bubbas to be processed outbound to one of three banks, the Bank of Cleveland, the Bank of Chicago and the Federal Reserve Bank of New York.

According to Lemont, when he arrived here on December 1st, he gave the receipt to our cage master, JoJo. Lemont alone with the garage crew unloaded 125 bags from his truck and that was it. Lemont then went out to finish his route for the day and then went home. The garage crew remembers unloading the bags but none of then had seen Lemont hand JoJo the receipt. Moreover, no one had seen what was in the bags, not even Lemont. The bags sat on the floor, within the caged in area of Bubbas garage, under the watchful eye of our in house cameras for four months."

Leila interrupted, "Wait a minute John, are you saying Lemont did not know what was in those 125 bags when he picked them up from Coins International?"

"That's correct Leila, he did not look within the bags but took it at face value that each 50 pound bag was full of pennies."

I jumped in, "John are you saying or implying that there may have been or may not have been money in those bags?"

"Frank, I am not implying anything, except to say we are not even sure if there was money in those bags at the time Lemont picked them up."

Leila came back, "So, John, it is possible that the crime could have occurred before Lemont picked up the bags of alleged money…correct?"

"Ahhh…Leila that's correct."

As I looked up from the floor, "John, it appears that a thorough investigation must start at Coins International and obviously there is more then one suspect?"

"That's right Frank, our estimate is approximately 100 suspects."

As I shook my head, "And the powers that be here at Bubbas Armored Car Corporate Headquarters has given us just one suspect, that's incredible."

"I don't make the rules Frank. That said, we don't even know if this is a conspiracy of many players or one person acting alone."

Leila stared at me and stated, "Are you thinking what I am thinking Frank?"

"If your're thinking Leila we are being played, your're right.

The analogy is this, in Africa when local tribesmen lead their herds across rivers infested with piranhas they throw one of their sickly cows downstream so the piranha's attack it and devour it while upstream the main herd crosses unscathed.

I know I'm going in harms way by saying what I am about to say, but John, I want it on the record and to be stated in the report that this is a totally irresponsible investigation."

Leila then stated, "Well, we are both out on a limb together Frank, but we're here let's run the test unless John wants to cancel it."

John explained, "You see, I am in a different situation then you two are, I work for the powers that be and they sign my check. I am not saying I agree with them or disagree with you but this is what they want. In any case, please run the examination and what happens, happens, okay?"

"Fine," I said as I looked back at Leila.

John then said, "Well, I'll leave you two to your investigation and I'll check on Lemont's status."

"Thank you," Leila stated.

As John left the conference room, I again stated my suspicions to Leila even though she knew where I was coming from.

"Leila, this is about integrity, it takes a whole life time to get an A+ rating from industry. Further, business and attorneys trust our good, fair and impartial judgment. That's why they call us from around the country for they trust and respect us for our confidentiality.

Have you ever heard Coco's speech on the type of people we examine?"

"Oh yes, I have." Leila affirmed.

"People respect us, Leila, because we are honest, straightforward and run a clean shop for we are driven by Christian principles though we walk through the valley of the sodomites, hominids, pagans and tattoo people. We bring justice to the afflicted and falsely accused and with the same vigor we hang the dirt bags. This is why the Investigators of Luna Pier have never had a complaint against them.

Enter these pimps who are attempting to compromise our integrity without care or remorse. You see Leila; the only thing that I, Frank Legion, have left in this world is my word and integrity.

So forgive me if I am old fashion or traditional but I resent being played."

"Frank, even though I worked Detroit vice I never lost my integrity or moral compass. The reason why I left vice, Frank, was after I lost my last two partners in a gunfight on a raid at a drug house, afterwards I just couldn't find anyone trustworthy to work with, except when I came to Luna Pier. It was the company's good reputation that brought me here, Frank. So I understand integrity and am aware of your concern. We're not going to throw an examination for these bums."

"Well, I am glad to hear that Leila, that we are both reading from the same sheet of music and are both on a straight and level playing field. Our mission is to catch the guilty parties and not crucify a sacrificial lamb."

"That's how I see it Frank."

"Good."

I looked for my Newport smokes in my briefcase because I knew I didn't have time to enjoy my Robusto cigar. At times I'd do anything for a drag.

Suddenly, John entered the conference room and introduced us to Lemont then left the room.

As Leila started her opening tactical gambit with Lemont I sat in the background and observed.

Leila stated, "Lemont we are going to read to you your rights because we want to make sure you understand them. If you agree with your rights then we will examine you, okay?"

Lemont replied, "Yes Ma`m."

Leila came back, "Lemont are you familiar with the reason why you are being polygraphed and the reason why you are here?"

"Yes, I am", Lemont spontaneously stated. "My supervisors somehow think I stole single-handedly $250,000 of pennies from this location after I dropped it off."

Leila, pretending to be occupied with a part on the polygraph instrument lifted her head and stated, "Well did you?"

Lemont laughing and rubbing his nose reiterated, "As I just said my supervisors somehow think I stole single-handedly $250,000 of pennies from this location…but I didn't."

Leila looked at him again with a cold stare, "Then who did Lemont?"

Lemont, pulling on his trousers pants stated, "How the hell do I know. I mean all I know is I brought the bags from Coins International to this location and gave, what's his face, the receipt of pickup and delivery.

Now I'm told da dude don't remember…what a joke."

I jumped in and asked, "Lemont did you help or plan with anyone to steal the money."

"Absolutely not, Mr...what's your name again?"

"Legion, Frank Legion."

"No, I didn't help or plan with anyone. Anyone could have taken the money after I dropped it off or when I was on vacation. It seems to me a whole lot of people should be polygraphed."

Thinking to myself, Lemont's answers were reasonable and were within specific parameters of truthful indications.

Leila replied, "Well, Lemont if you feel that you're being set up for the fall, then why are you taking this polygraph examination?"

"Well I asked for it because I am tired of being suspected of being a thief, that's why."

"Lemont, have you ever been arrested for a felony or involved in any type of theft in your past?" Leila asked.

Lemont answered, "No, dey wouldn't have hired me. Ah never been arrested."

"You trying to tell me Lemont, that not connected with this case you never stolen anything in your life?" I interjected.

Lemont stated, "Ah mean as a kid I stole things but nothing big, you know?"

"Are you listening Lemont, didn't Leila just ask you if you were involved in any theft of any kind in your past?" I yelled back.

"Well ya, but, I guess ah misunstood da question?" Lemont replied.

"Your going to pay attention to my questions from now on, right Lemont?" Leila asked.

"Yaah." Lemont answered.

Did you steal any of the approximate $250,000 in coins from Coins International?" Leila asked.

"Heck no, you think ah be working here in dis joint if ah did," Lemont replied. (Laughing)

"Do you know right now where any of that stolen $250,000 in coins are?" Leila asked.

"No, but ah wish ah did, that's a lot of money" Lemont replied.

"Did you plan with anyone to steal any of the approximate $250,000 in coins from Coins International?"

"No," Lemont replied.

"Did you help in any way to steal the approximate $250,000 in coins from Coins International?" asked Leila.

"No.", replied Lemont.

"Do you know who stole the money Lemont? Not who you think but do you know, that is, eyeball present," Leila asked.

"I don't know that either," Lemont stated.

"Those are the questions we are going to ask you Lemont. How do you think the test will come out?" I asked.

"If dis thing works right, I should come out good," Lemont shot back.

"Those are the questions we are going to ask you on the exam, do you except them?" Leila questioned.

"Yah, I accept them," Lemont replied.

"Who do you think stole the money Lemont?" I queried.

"Well," Lemont responded, "That armored cars from another company dropped of their load to the cage master JoJo and took the wrong load out."

"Are you saying Lemont that personnel from another armored car company could enter the secured caged area and take a non-designated load out? Doesn't the cage master know who's coming and going and what they're taking?" Leila questioned.

"No, mistakes are made all the time here and armored cars have to return back to their prior destination and switch their incorrect bags for the proper ones," Lemont explained.

"Oh man", I said, "This is sounding more and more like Abbot and Costello comical, "Who's on First." This was an accident waiting to happen…what a mess."

"Did any banks receive the coins in question from any armored car company?" Leila asked.

"Nope, it's gone" Lemont replied.

As I looked at Leila, I stated, "How can someone run an operation like this, either the people at the top are clueless or it's being deliberately run this way for someone's benefit.

Lets test Lemont, Leila, and get him out of here."

Leila laughing, "I agree."

As Lemont settled in his hardback chair, I observed no negative body language or countermeasures present. Lemont may not have been the sharpest tool in the shed but from his entire exterior posturing, he looked "Good to go."

After a battery of polygraph examinations, Lemont's polygrams looked consistent with truthfulness. Leila also concurred with my findings and she informed Lemont of our conclusion.

"Ah, knew ah was innocent but ah can't say that for everyone working here..ya know? Everyone should have to take dis test," stated Lemont.

As Lemont shook our hands and thanked us for clearing him and saving his job, he departed the room and headed back to his work detail.

At this time while we were cleaning up the area and gathering our charts and polygraph equipment, I could see a fat balding man, mid forties in a tan suit, approaching our location.

Intuitively, I knew and suspected that this man was one of the Chief Executive Officers wondering about the results of Lemont. But experience has shown me, again, that many times a perpetrator of a particular crime returns to the scene of the crime to, "Check things out."

Though in reality and not conclusive, it was an indicator of deception for the perpetrator wants to know if we "law dogs" are off his trail or still sniffing."

And we were still sniffing!

In my mind, here came one of the point men or advance guard for the conspirators.

"Mr. Frank Legion how are you, I'm, Mr. Paris, the vice president of Bubbas Armored Car Company."

As I looked at his phony smile, which had as much sincerity as a "Hollywood kiss," I shook his hand and stated, "I'm fine sir and Leila here is my associate."

"Hello Leila, it is a pleasure to meet you both. I understand you administered a polygraph examination on one of our employees?"

"That is correct", Leila stated, "As a matter of fact we have completed the examination and Lemont, your employee, past with flying colors."

At that moment in time, as I studied Mr. Paris's face and body language, I could see his tanning booth "styling tan" turned from bottled orange to ashen gray skin in a heartbeat of time.

My, my I said to myself, he just realized he had to put "Plan B" in play and here he thought he out foxed us. But we piranhas didn't take his bait, so I awaited silently for this dumb and plumb, Mr. Peabody, with the same physical makeup of the zoo keeper in a Dr. Seuss child's book to make his opening move.

Then with an unbelievable shocked look on his ashen face, Mr. Paris shot back, "He did? I was certain he wouldn't. That can't be, you must be mistaken."

As Leila looked at me as if with telepathy we both understood that Mr. Paris had just pissed away his money for one investigation that only a lame brain would have fallen for.

Leila stated, "No, Mr. Paris, we both reached the same conclusion independently of each other and our application of the polygraph technique was "spot on". No errors or mistakes on this end. It is our understanding there are 15 to approximately 100 people who could be likely suspects. Will we be testing anybody else Mr. Paris?"

Mr. Paris raising his voice and thinking we were one of his lapdogs went for the high ground.

"No, you examiners have made a mistake, Lemont had to do it," Mr. Paris angrily shot back.

I jumped in and figuratively speaking threw this Peabody off the high ground and established a defensive perimeter immediately.

"Again, Mr. Paris, we made no mistakes and the examination was conducted under exact American Polygraph Bureau standards. Moreover, the questions were directly focused on the issue, which your own security personnel wanted us to ask.

They even informed us that their questions came down from the top, which infers you or the man over you wanted them asked," as I stared down Mr. Paris.

Both Leila and I knew where this whole argument was going. Moreover we knew we would lose the business contract with these "tobacco-spitting hacks" who were hoping to control and influence our outcome.

Mr. Paris, regrouping and charging back up the hill in a desperate attempt to regain the high ground stated, "Well, I don't care what security says, I run the business here and I didn't want these questions asked at all. I want different questions asked pertinent to this case and I will give you the questions I want you to ask."

"Mr. Paris," I stated, "The examination is concluded, the official questions have been asked and Lemont has passed his examination.… period.

That said, will we be examining any more of the possible suspects in this case, including yourself, Mr. Paris, or is this the end of this incomplete investigation?"

Mr. Paris facial color had gone from ashen gray to fire engine red stated angrily, "What do you mean me? What are you talking about? Is that what Lemont stated?"

"No", I shot back, Lemont did not say that, but during the course of our investigation employees believe management concocted this whole event by throwing us some young black man who didn't have the means or the resources to pull this off."

"Well, I am not taking the test with either of you or anyone else as a matter-of-fact. Nor will I hire your firm anymore," Mr. Paris angrily replied.

"Well, Mr. Paris," Leila explained, "Our business is done here and we will send you the report and the bill tomorrow."

Mr. Paris, not satisfied with our responses stated, "I will not accept your report, nor will I read it and neither am I going to pay you."

I struck back, "Mr. Paris, you can have it your way, for tomorrow I will file a small claims request at the local district court against your firm for failure to pay for services outstanding. At that time as we can stand before the judge and a full courtroom of people, I will explain in great detail how you believe a black employee, acting alone, stole 3 tons of pennies right under your noses in full view of your employees and all the floor cameras that just mysteriously went out of service."

Mr. Paris stormed out of the office and within a few minutes a carrier returned with a check and gave it to Leila for polygraph services rendered.

As Leila and I walked out of the building, Leila looked at me and stated, "You know Frank, we did the right thing but it is not appreciated. It kind of takes the wind out of your sail."

"No, Leila," as I stopped and took one of the briefcases from her arms, "We did good today, we freed an innocent man and kept wickedness at bay. We held the line and justice was served.

How about some dinner?"

"Sounds good, Frank."

## Chapter 13 - Where's the stash?

After Leila headed back to Luna Pier with the report, Coco notified me that Sheila, one of our field investigators was working alone on a marijuana case involving a number of men in Richmond, Indiana. Sheila had requested assistance from Coco stating she did not want to enter their home without backup or support personnel.

Like most of us investigators, we were always uncomfortable with people who were involved in narcotics whether legal or not. There was just something about these people that we didn't trust and could be placed in harms way in a New York second.

On approach, Sheila vectored me in to her location, which was a small coffee shop on the outskirts of Richmond. I found Sheila sitting outside at a picnic table reviewing her case.

I asked her whatever happened to her assigned police case regarding a lieutenant shaking his subordinates officers penis instead of their hands as a greeting.

Sheila informed me that Coco just advised her to waive off the case of the "penis grabber" for the moment, for the police officers (victims) are all tied up testifying in a murder trial.

"Frank, the switch came right from the top, apparently from Big Don at the Maumee Bay office. He informed Coco that he would handle the money matters of the original case and when it's resolved he'll reassign it to me. So, I assume when the police officers are clear of their murder trial and front the money, I'll be reassigned."

So Coco redirected me here to Richmond, Indiana regarding a case of 75 plants of medical marijuana allegedly being stolen from a legal growers place of abode."

Sheila further explained, "According to Coco, the plants are estimated at $40,000 dollars along with about $35,000 to $50,000 dollars in plant equipment being stolen. The plants were apparently cut at the stems leaving just the stumps, while the rest of the house was left unscathed.

The grower is very concerned that if the Fed`s get wind of this incident they will swoop in on his alleged operation and drag him into court for possible prosecution.

Moreover, the grower was equally concerned that he could not adequately supply his legally designated patients who would complain to the authorities.

Funny thing, Frank, the culprits who broke into the house/garage walked right by about $10,000 in new computer hardware and stereo equipment without even touching them."

"Wow…. how many known suspects are involved in this case, Sheila?"

"Well, what I know of right now, Frank, there are only five suspects who were aware that there was marijuana in the growers home.  All five wanted to take a polygraph examination to clear themselves from suspicions or allegations that they were involved in the breaking and entering and/or theft of the marijuana.

The word on the street, Frank, is that all six of these individuals are long time friends and the grower is just devastated that he was betrayed by boyhood buddy's going back almost 30 years.

My own personal take on this matter, Frank, is that we are on a mercy mission for the growers clients who are in dire need of pain killer medication.  So Big Don wants us to nail these dirt bags that stole pain relieving medicine from terminally cancer patients."

"Sheila, apparently Big Don has a soft touch after all for I can't remember a time when he would pass up business money for a mercy mission.  Shows you that you don't know a person until the fat lady sings.

Okay, Sheila, can you bring me up to speed on some of the legal particulars regarding Medical Marijuana, that is, from a legal standpoint?  I mean I'm clueless at the moment, though I know polygraph examiners acting, as agents for their clients should become familiar with the growing body of law regarding medical marijuana.

Yet, then again Sheila, how can we be cognizant of everything regarding the law without corporation counsel at our beckon call to brief us continuously.  You know, I debated this numerous times with Ed and Big Don that we should have a paid attorney on staff who could keep us abreast of new and developing legal matters that concern us.  But the bosses feel that the attorneys want too big a cut into corporate profits."

"Well, this is what I know Frank, for the law is changing almost daily.  As things now stand approximately 14 states permit the use of medical marijuana.  Yet the Federal Controlled Substance Act prohibits the distribution and possession of marijuana with no medical exclusion. Moreover, doctors and other licensed health care professionals do not write prescriptions for the use of marijuana but rather make recommendations that the use of marijuana may alleviate or lessen the symptoms involving pain or discomfort."

"Okay, Sheila, I'm listening."

"Apparently, Frank, according to government data there are approximately 17 million marijuana users in the United States. Of that, 600,000 users have been given medical recommendations by their health care provider. Marijuana is a Schedule I substance which is authorized primarily for research purposes and is not supervised. While Scheduled II drugs are prescribed and are required to be monitored.

As we know current marijuana use among the population is on the rise and it's medical benefit is questionable. I guess people need some kind of relief from the failing job market and bleak economic recovery."

"Sheila, most people on the stuff just can't face the hard edge of reality and seek comfort in the realm of Alice in Wonderland. But then again some people are like vegetable plants in my garden, that is, they cannot produce even under the best of conditions and should not belong among those that do."

"Eugenics, Frank?"

"I'm sorry, I was thinking aloud, Sheila."

"Sure Frank, why don't you tell us what you really feel about things in general?" (Laughing)

"Ahhh, Sheila …I wouldn't want to bore you with my, "Dudley Do Right" attitude."

"I think Frank, our opening hand should be to try and find out which of these five examinee's have a marijuana habit and if any of them have arrest or jail time for distributing marijuana or narcotics."

"That sounds good, Sheila, plus run a background check to determine if any of them have a prior history for being arrested for breaking and entering, home invasion and theft. Then check to see if they have a current job or history for bouncing bad checks."

"Sounds like we have a plan Frank."

"It works for me, Sheila, why don't we run the five exams over the next two days?"

"Sounds good, I'll do a background check on them and inform the owner that we will run the exams over the course of two days."

"Make sure Sheila, that all the examinee's have been informed prior to the examination to be at said location at the proper time and date. For if they skip out for no justifiable reason they could be our culprits who have failed themselves by default.

Lastly, if they all pass and there are no extraneous outside variables then the owner himself must be tested in order to verify his truthfulness regarding this matter."

"I agree, Frank, I'll get back with you tomorrow regarding any loss ends that may arise and I'll schedule the exams the following day."

"Good, stay in touch Sheila, and stay frosty."

The following day Sheila called me and confirmed again that there would be five examinees for testing and the owner would pay the bill. I advised Sheila that if any of the examinees refused to release the polygraph results to the owner it would be his lost since the law regarding the results protects the examinee and not who pays the bill.

Sheila stated all examinees were made aware of this and all agreed to have the owner sent the results. They all allege they had nothing to hide and did not want to jeopardize their long friendship with the owner. I informed Sheila, that's good and hopefully all the examinees will pass making our work rewarding by protecting and clearing the innocent from false allegations and suspicions. Sheila and I agreed to start the exams tomorrow at first light in order to finish by mid afternoon.

The following day Sheila and I met at the Indiana location, which looked like a safe house for some fugitive from justice. When I asked why we were taken to this desolate location, the owner stated he did not want the tests overheard by members of his family. Sheila asked the owner whatever happened to the private conference room, he claimed he had at a respectable hotel that was just around the corner from his house? At that time the owner did not have an answer, so I asked the owner if we were going into a drug den. He then replied, "No, my operation is totally legitimate and I have the papers to prove it."

After review of the papers and stepping away for a moment, I asked Sheila, "Look, I'm no attorney and don't claim to be one, but these papers could be forged and we could be going in harms way.

I forgot to ask you, are you packen? Because if your not I have a five round police snub revolver in my briefcase in case things turn from bad to worst."

"Hell yes I'm packen, Frank," Sheila replied. "I have a Browning .25 caliber with six rounds."

"Good to hear that, I thought they carried eight rounds Sheila?"

"Frank, don't be a smart ass, hell, I can't remember. Either way, it's too late now for it's just you and me against six of them if things go wrong."

"I know Sheila, damn, I'm getting to old for this kind of stuff. Here we are on a dirt road in the middle of nowhere, between somewhere and elsewhere, walking into an Indiana farmhouse with who knows who?

Imagine the general populace thinks polygraph examiners work out of a safe and secure business environment for their bread and butter...*nothing could be farther from the truth for we go in harms way every day!*

Hell, I can't remember a day when I felt safe and secure.... but it's sure been interesting traveling and meeting the complete strata of the American people.

I'll call Coco and speak encrypted to her as to what we're doing."

"I think that would be a safe thing to do," Sheila replied.

As we walked back to the owner, I got Coco on the phone and stated within earshot of the owner, "We're green for five, stand down the dogs!"

The owner and a couple examinees looked at me inquisitively.... *but got the drift.*

Sheila and I decided to go with the standard relevant questions and interlace them together and overlap their parameters in order to find any semblance of guilty knowledge:

(1) On the date in question, do you know who stole the marijuana plants from a house on Anne Street? (NO)

(2) On the date in question, did you steal any marijuana plants from the house on Anne Street? (NO)

(3) On the date in question, did you plan with anyone to steal any marijuana plants from the house on Anne Street? (NO)

(4) On the date in question, did you help to steal any marijuana plants from the house on Anne Street? (NO)

(5) Do you know right now where any of the missing marijuana plants are that were stolen from the house on Anne Street? (NO)

After we completed the examinations we analyzed the charts and much to our surprise the first three examinees were totally truthful and turned out to be real patriotic Americans who took their long-term relationship with the owner seriously. We found that refreshing especially when they told us they wanted to join the Marine Corps.

So I informed them of just about everything I knew to hopefully improve their success if they were so inclined to do so.

I couldn't help but think to myself, was I ever that young. As I reflected back what else could working class white boys do but to serve their country or become cops.

After the third test, the owner who had been outside throughout the duration, apparently left after the third examinee passed his exam completely.

As we were finishing up, the owner called my cell phone whereby he informed me that examinee number four and number five went to an Indiana college football game instead of making themselves available for their examination.

I asked the owner, "Didn't you tell me there would be five examinations and were not all five examinees notified to be here to take their exams?"

The owner replied, "Yes I did, but if anybody did not show you would still be paid full boat."

"Yes, Sheila, made me aware of that conversation but the issue in question, sir, is not money but completing a full and thorough investigation, if you get my drift?"

"Yes I got it," replied the owner.

I explained again, "Understand, that if all the known players who are allegedly involved in this theft of medical marijuana are not tested then we examiners cannot bring closure to this problem.

That is, these two individuals and yourself included should be cognizant that if the Fed's get a hold of this matter in question, you and your two friends will be polygraphed to eliminate the possibility of an inside job. I hope you're aware of that?"

"I am," the owner quietly replied.

"Well, seeing your aware of that, Sheila and myself want to inform you that these three subjects we just tested passed their polygraphs examinations without a glitch. Furthermore, I would recommend that you keep them as trusting friends."

The owner warmly replied, "I thank you sir, and if you would kindly lock the door on your departure, it would be most appreciated."

"You can considerate it done sir and thanks for the business." Though intuitively I said to myself that there is more to this story. For I know the Federal law dogs are stiffing and their coming…. but it's his money and ass on the line.

As Sheila and I walked away we decided before heading back to Luna Pier, we would head out to a Coney Island to get a couple dogs smothered with everything and a cold beer or two…or three.

Suddenly my cell phone rang, from Luna Pier.

"Frank, it's Coco, don't unpack your clothes just yet. Big Don wants to see you tomorrow at his Maumee Bay Investigative office."

"You're kidding?" I stated.

"No, there's a big caseload Frank, you up for it?"

After hesitating for a period of time, I stated, "Yes, I'll be there."

\*\*\*

9 780615 953076